"This book is readable, understandable, informative, and greatly needed for church ministries to the military and their families. I highly recommend this book."
—James A. Almquist, Lutheran Parish Pastor, retired; Chair, Ministry to the Military, Calvary Lutheran Church, Golden Valley, MN; Chaplain (COL) USAR, retired

"Whether a church is near a military base, has only a family or two with a deployed member, or desires to be more aware of what others in our communities are going through, *Beyond the Yellow Ribbon* is a must read!"
—Sally Dyck, Resident Bishop Minnesota Annual Conference of The United Methodist Church

"David and Darlene have given us a powerful and comprehensive glimpse into the lives of the military men and women who serve us. The book is filled with helpful suggestions for ministering to our servicemen and servicewomen and their families. After reading this book you will have a deeper appreciation for their sacrifice and a greater resolve to help the church 'be the church' for those who serve on our behalf."
—Matthew A. Thomas, Bishop, Free Methodist Church North America

"A must-read resource for civilian clergy and chaplains of all faith groups that can help them and members of their congregations reach out to returning combat veterans and their families. This insightful work should prove effective in lowering high divorce and suicide rates among those who know from experience that war is hell."
—Gene Thomas Gomulka, Captain, Chaplain Corps, U.S. Navy (Ret), Author of *The Survival Guide for Marriage in the Military*

Beyond the Yellow Ribbon

Ministering to Returning Combat Veterans

David A. Thompson
and
Darlene F. Wetterstrom

Abingdon Press
Nashville

BEYOND THE YELLOW RIBBON
MINISTERING TO RETURNING COMBAT VETERANS

Copyright © 2009 by Abingdon Press

This book is printed on acid-free paper.

Library of Congress Cataloging-in-Publication Data

Thompson, David A., 1946-
    Beyond the yellow ribbon : ministering to returning combat veterans / David A. Thompson and Darlene F. Wetterstrom.
        p.   cm.
    Includes bibliographical references (p.   ) and index.
    ISBN 978-0-687-46575-0 (binding: pbk. : alk. paper)
    1. Church work with veterans—United States. I. Wetterstrom, Darlene F. II. Title.
    BV4459.T56 2009
    259.088'35500973—dc22

                                                                        2009032394

Unless otherwise indicated, all Scripture quotations are taken from the New Revised Standard Version of the Bible, copyright 1989, Division of Christian Education of the National Council of the Churches of Christ in the United States of America. Used by permission. All rights reserved.

Scripture marked (NIV) taken from the Holy Bible, NEW INTERNATIONAL VERSION®. Copyright © 1973, 1978, 1984 by International Bible Society. All rights reserved throughout the world. Used by permission of International Bible Society.

Scripture quotations marked (NEB) are from *The New English Bible.* © The Delegates of the Oxford University Press and The Syndics of the Cambridge University Press 1961, 1970. Reprinted by permission.

Scripture quotations marked (GNT) are from the Good News Translation in Today's English Version- Second Edition © 1992 by American Bible Society. Used by Permission.

09 10 11 12 13 14 15 16 17 18—10 9 8 7 6 5 4 3 2 1
MANUFACTURED IN THE UNITED STATES OF AMERICA

Contents

Introduction

Beyond the Yellow Ribbon: Ministering to Returning Combat Veterans will equip your church to welcome veterans home from war.

Military life is not easy on service members or their families! It takes some pretty hardy and resilient people to manage successfully going off to war and coming home again. Many veterans make it through this transition and go on to lead productive lives in our communities, but that is not always the case.

Some veterans are broken in body or spirit by their wartime experiences and struggle for years trying to put their lives back together. Long after hanging up their uniforms, some get captured by postwar addictions. Other veterans lose their place in the world of work and struggle to find good jobs. Couples must cope with readjusting to each other, and children often become estranged from parents after long absences.

Beyond the Yellow Ribbon is designed to heighten awareness of this hidden community of veterans and their families embedded in our congregations and in our neighborhoods. They are often overlooked in the personal ministry plans of clergy or in the outreach efforts of congregational care ministries. The book identifies specific needs of veterans and their families and discusses creative ways churches can minister to them.

Some individuals mentioned in the book are composites of several people, or whole groups of people we have known or whose stories we have heard, who illustrate the issue at hand. We have taken great care to avoid identifying these people in ways that would cause any harm or embarrassment to them.

We will occasionally make references to "soldiers" in a generic sense to include all service members of the armed forces: Army, Navy, Air Force, Marine Corps, National Guard, and Coast Guard. This economy of words is not meant to ignore service members from other services. Such a device merely helps avoid having to identify each service member of each component as "soldier, sailor, airman, marine, or guard personnel." When we address a specific service, however, the proper term for that service will be used.

We honor all veterans who are serving or have served their country in uniform. We pay tribute to their families who managed the home front during their soldier's service. We also want to say a special word of thanks to our spouses, Judy Thompson and Dan Wetterstrom, who read the manuscript and provided helpful editorial assistance.

On this Memorial Day, we remember veterans who made the ultimate sacrifice for our country. God bless their memory and allow their sacrificial spirit to live on in our lives! We also remember family members who have borne the special grief that never goes away, of laying a fallen soldier to rest in a garden of stone. May the hope of the resurrection and the peace and grace of God bring solace and comfort to these Gold Star Families who mourn today.

David A. Thompson
Darlene F. Wetterstrom

CHAPTER ONE

Soldiers and Their Families in Our Midst: Who Are These People?

Love your neighbor as yourself. —*Matthew 22:39*

Janice sat quietly in the back of the church, her head bowed and hands clasped. She tried to focus on Pastor Jim's Memorial Day sermon about remembrance, but it was difficult to do. As she peered out over the congregants, she wondered, "How many besides me in this church have been touched by war?" She already knew of some. She glanced over at Mrs. McGonagall. Her first husband had been killed in the Korean War and as a young bride she had grieved for the lifelong marriage she would never have. Janice saw two high school boys sitting near the front of the church between their grandparents. Their mother and father were both deployed to Iraq, and they were now being raised by their grandparents, who long ago thought they were through raising kids. In the pew across the aisle sat Lisa, whose husband, Bill, had gone to Vietnam right out of high school. Bill came back wounded and confused. They had tried to rebuild their life together but it did not work. Eventually they divorced and went their separate ways.

Janice closed her eyes tight and thought of her own circumstance. Her son, Tim, had returned home from a

1

sixteen-month tour in Afghanistan more than ten months ago. Tim's wife, Cindy, and their three young children had been anxious to get him home safe and sound. She had helped them prepare for the homecoming. They had purchased balloons and ribbons and invited family and friends to welcome him back. The children had on hero T-shirts and the tables were laden with food. But it had gone off wrong from the beginning. Tim sat in a corner of the room and ate little food. He shrugged off most questions and escaped to his bedroom as soon as he could. Janice was sure it had to do with exhaustion and was confident things would get better soon.

But they had not gotten better; in fact, they had gotten worse. Tim seemed to be in a fog. He rarely talked, and when he did, it was usually to berate one of their children. He had trouble sleeping and seemed incapable of making even a small decision. He did go back to work, but that took up most of his energy. The only time he seemed energized was when he was with one of his fellow soldiers. But that lasted only as long as the visit. And then he was back to his withdrawn self.

Janice was unsure what to do. As a Christian she looked to her church for guidance and support. But did her church understand the issues facing military families? Could she go to Pastor Jim and ask him for help? And what type of help could he give? And what about Tim? Would he be willing to seek out help? And how would the church know what type of help they could offer Tim or any military family?

Janice tried to educate others on the struggles facing military families, but she soon came to realize that specific information about who service members are, why they join the military service, and the struggles they face are often met with misinformation and outright guesses. Many people listened to her but still asked the question, *And who are these people?*

Who are these people? can often be followed up with a silent question, *And why should we care?* Why should

Americans care about soldiers and their families? And specifically why should church people care about them? Military service members make up less than one-half of 1 percent of our population. In most communities this translates into very few service members attending our churches.

And yet soldiers are our neighbors, even though many of us see military families as a subculture with whom we have little connection or interest in becoming acquainted. Jesus' parable of the good Samaritan, found in Luke 10:30-37, talks about a man on a journey who was accosted by thieves, beaten, robbed, and left for dead. In the narrative one person after another passed him without helping him, either being too busy to stop or fearful of what obligations would be involved if they did stop. It wasn't that they did not love their neighbors—just not *this* neighbor, this person they did not know or understand.

The Samaritan, in contrast, stopped and helped the wounded man. Confronted with need, this man opened himself up to helping someone whom he did not know and who was different from himself. In the end he went to great lengths and expense to help someone in need.

Helmut Thielike, a German Lutheran theologian, in his book *The Waiting Father* reminds us that the essence of this parable is that "our neighbor chooses us" (not that we choose our neighbors) as he or she lies beaten and broken and in need beside the road we walk. Thielike asks, "To whom am I a neighbor? Who is laid at my door? Who is expecting help from me and looks upon me as his neighbor?" (Thielike, 1959, p. 168).

Many soldiers and their family members may be like the man beside the road, in need of us being "neighborly to them in Jesus' name." But to help means we need to have a degree of understanding. Pastors and lay leaders need to be sensitive to the struggles found within their congregations and communities, whether it is alcoholism, divorce, loneliness, or broken relationships. While church leaders cannot be expected to solve all of their congregants' problems, they can be expected to have a broader understanding so that they can minister more effectively.

This book, *Beyond the Yellow Ribbon: Ministering to Returning Combat Veterans,* enables readers to have a deeper understanding and appreciation of some significant struggles soldiers and their families face. But understanding is not enough. Understanding must directly translate into helping others. Churches have a mission to reach out to the lost, the lonely, and the hurting. And as they reach out to help others, they will find soldiers and their families in need of services and support. This book will help you offer that support.

They Are Us

There is a military myth that states, "The military takes care of its own." The premise for this myth is that soldiers, airmen, marines, sailors, and coast guard personnel are part of a bigger system that excludes civilians and embraces service members. The idea is that when a recruit signs up to serve, the recruit gets a new family in the bargain. The idea is that this new family will take care of the service member's needs. It very rarely works out that way.

The military does indeed provide amenities to its service members. They are paid a salary. They receive training for their MOS (military operation specialty). They are fed and provided uniforms. They are given housing. But that does not mean that every issue is addressed or cared for. And it does not mean that service members are no longer part of the civilian world.

Indeed, the civilian world seems to automatically exclude them. They put service members on a different plane or give them a different status. Ask most civilians about service members and they will almost inevitably say, "Oh, they are heroes." When pressed to say why they are heroes, civilians will respond, "Because they have sacrificed so much for our country." Asked who takes care of or supports these service members, most civilians will answer, "The military takes care of them."

Soldiers endure hardships, no doubt. They are separated from family for extended periods of time. They are deployed to different and at times dangerous locations throughout the world. They are limited in their choices and have to obey their commanders. But does becoming a soldier mean becoming a hero?

Most soldiers resent being labeled a hero. Most soldiers would tell a well-wisher that they are not heroes but rather are "just doing their job." They are processing payroll or fixing planes or driving trucks. They have paid responsibilities and work goals. They have timelines and deadlines and projects. "Just doing their job" is a phrase that applies to most adults. Don't most adults get up each morning and head off to work? Some jobs are tedious; some are exciting. Some take considerable skill, while others take minimal thinking. But most workers end their day with the knowledge that they were "doing their job."

When we elevate all soldiers to hero status, we risk separating them from our shared life experiences. They become "them" and we are "us." We aren't one of them, because they are heroes. We aren't one of them; they belong to the military. The military "owns" them. And if they belong to someone else, they are someone else's concern. When we hear of their problems, we can minimize or ignore them. After all, they are not us.

Still, heroes do exist in the military. Many honorable men and women have performed incredible acts of bravery that resulted in great injury or death. These soldiers have earned their medals and crosses for bravery. Our country owes them our gratitude. But heroes exist in other places too. Daily, there are news clips of firefighters storming burning buildings or a neighbor dashing in front of a car to grab a wandering toddler. Heroes exist outside of the military. All of us are capable of heroic acts, but few of us will be called upon to perform one.

We share similar traits and values with service members. We marry; they marry. We have children; they have children. They get sad; we get sad. They struggle; we struggle. It is important that we recognize that while differences do exist, so do similarities. There is no "they" and "us." We are they. Service members come from our state, our community, and our families. We should not allow ourselves to place them in their own sealed category. Once we categorize them, we run the risk of ignoring them. And when we ignore them, they suffer. They don't want to be excluded; they don't want to be different. They are soldiers, but they are also human. They have some unique experiences, but all humans have unique experiences. We need to understand their uniqueness while still acknowledging their sameness.

What Is Unique about Service Members

Each of the five branches of service that make up our military has its own specialty. The Army focuses on ground missions, the Navy roams the seas, and the Air Force defends air space. The Marines are basically the "air/land expeditionary force," and the Coast Guard is used in law enforcement, boating safety, and illegal immigration control. While each branch differs from the others, they are all united as the military and ultimately are under the president of the United States, the commander-in-chief.

Service members can be on active duty, in the National Guard, or in the Reserves. When most Americans think of service members, they conjure up pictures of military bases. There are more than 200 bases in the United States. Some bases are small, like Fort McCoy, Wisconsin, and some are very large, such as Fort Bragg in Fayetteville, North Carolina. Military bases are in essence "gated communities" that provide housing, schools, medical services, and support to active duty soldiers. Active duty families who live on bases often feel that they are removed from civilian communities, and in fact do feel that most of their needs are met "on base."

Active duty soldiers and their families can leave the civilian world behind when they flash their military identification card to the guards at entrance gates. Once they enter their base, they speak a similar language and understand each other's world. But their world is also influenced by the civilian world. They watch the same television shows; they eat the same foods; they buy the same clothes; and they study the same subjects in school. But because they are "behind walls," they are often seen as "different" and "not part of us."

National Guard and Reservists are even more confusing for civilians to understand. Although those terms often are used interchangeably, they are different. The National Guard falls under the jurisdiction of the state governor. The National Guard is used during civil unrest and disasters in their state, and they are to be available for federal active duty far away from their home state. Once they become deployed, they are under the jurisdiction of the federal government. National Guard families live in both worlds. They often have civilian jobs but drill (train) one weekend a month and two weeks during the year.

National Guard members usually serve with residents of their states, while Reservists fall under the federal government authority and serve with soldiers from all over the United States. However, they too have their feet in both the military and the civilian worlds. They often have a regular weekday or five-day-a-week job and drill or train one weekend per month. Reservists and guard personnel describe themselves as members of the military, but often their families don't see themselves as military families unless their spouse or partner deploys. And then they are thrust into a military system they often don't understand or fully appreciate.

The Adventure of Being in the Military

For many Americans the idea of being in the military conjures up images of adventure. As teenagers move toward

7

their high school graduation, they are faced with the ongoing dilemma of *What am I going to do after I graduate?* For many kids it means going to college; for others it may be a trade school or a waiting job. But for a small percentage of students, there is the lure of the military.

Joining the military often allows men and women to see and experience things they would never have the opportunity to do as civilians. They can visit exotic countries, learn to fly amazing planes, sail on ships, or test their endurance running as soldiers or marines miles on end with heavy backpacks. They get to meet fellow service personnel from all over the United States. Many also feel a patriotic duty to serve their county and help keep it safe. The military offers men and women a sense of duty and mission that they might otherwise not have. In exchange for this adventure, service members allow the military to dictate what they will do, where they will live, and how much they will be paid. For many service members there is comfort and relief in not having to make all of those decisions on their own. This is particularly true with active duty soldiers.

Most National Guard members and Reservists have full-time civilian jobs. But once they are deployed, they become an active duty soldier. They become "fully military" and put their civilian life on hold. Many National Guard and Reservists join the military for part-time service and some extra income. In addition, they may also receive money for college as well as a bonus for signing up.

How does the military adventure affect the family members who stay home—the spouses or partners who stay at home working full-time jobs? How does the military adventure affect the mother of four elementary school children who has just been told her husband will be gone for over one year? Most families look for pay-offs and balance as they assess their roles and military involvement.

Active duty families often feel they have a better and clearer pay-off than those who are in the Guards or

Reserves. Many active duty military families put up with the long separations and frequent moves because there is a reward for doing so. Active duty soldiers can retire after twenty years of service on half base pay according to rank (or three-fourths basic pay for thirty years of service). For a soldier who enters into the full-time military service at age twenty, that means he or she can retire at the relatively young age of forty. Many soldiers are deployed to areas where their family can join them. Some military families are stationed, at government expense, in beautiful Hawaii or other exotic places in Europe or Asia. The children might go to school and receive medical care on base. Families on bases often form strong and quick friendships with other military families, because they have learned to adapt to new situations and are able to reach out to others who share very similar experiences.

For families in the National Guard or Reserves, the payoff can seem questionable or ambiguous at best. Guard and Reserve families live in the community and not on a base. They are not usually in a position to take their family along on a deployment. That means the family does not get to move to exciting places or mingle with other military families. It also means that many National Guard and Reserve families are left feeling quite alone and isolated when their spouse or partner goes on a deployment.

Deployments are difficult for active duty families as well as families in the Reserves and National Guard. All families struggle with this, but how they struggle is directly related to the support they receive while their loved one is deployed. Active duty soldiers can usually find built-in support through their bases. For the National Guard and Reserves, support is harder to find and less likely to be effective. Churches can help bridge that gap. They can be an ongoing support system for all military families, but especially to the families who are community based and who are not sure where to turn for help.

9

What Military Families Want Us to Know

Military families, be it active duty, National Guard, or Reserves, want us to see them as people first. Yes, they wear uniforms with badges and awards many of us will never understand. Yes, they have acronyms and ranks that baffle most civilians. And yet they intermingle with us on a daily basis. They share the same hopes and dreams we do. But how they obtain their hopes and dreams is often determined significantly by the military.

The military is formed by taking the "average citizen" and making him or her into a soldier. This means the average citizen has to learn how to "think like a soldier" and be obedient to superiors. This strong chain of command allows the military to function. The average citizen has to learn how to obey without question, because a soldier in combat cannot afford to question the command he was just given. His life and the lives of his fellow soldiers depend on his prompt response.

Learning to obey begins when a civilian enters military basic training, affectionately known as boot camp. Orders are given by drill instructors and the recruit is expected to obey them. If she chooses not to obey, there are instant and severe consequences. Boot camp is used to transform raw recruits from civilians into soldiers, so it is hard and challenges the recruit's mental and physical endurance. Its goal is to force the recruit to give up his or her individual identity in order to form a new identity as part of the unit. To be effective, a unit needs to be a collection of soldiers who think and act in unison.

A recruit is slowly transformed into a solider with a new identity shared with the unit. But her parents, siblings, spouse, and children are not being changed into soldiers. They don't have the same transforming experience and are able to keep their same identity. The family member they tearfully waved goodbye to for boot camp is the not the same person they welcome home. The recruit is now a soldier who belongs to a larger system. This transforming experience is not a shared experience. Boot camp starts the military journey in which the soldier has to navigate two worlds, the world of the military and the civilian world he shares with his family.

At times these worlds coexist peacefully. When a soldier is not deployed, she often goes to a job much like most people go to a job. She usually comes home at the end of the day, just like her family members. But when there is a deployment, the military world takes over and the needs and wants of the family often take on a secondary status. When a soldier gets the order to deploy, he does not say, "Well, I am not sure I am in a good place to go to Iraq. Perhaps someone else can go for me this time and I will be ready to go the next time the unit deploys." A soldier is taught to obey, and if he is told that he has three weeks to get ready for a deployment, when the time comes he is ready. If he is told that he is now being moved to a new base, he gets ready to move. The soldier does not question but obeys.

This is often in direct contrast with the civilian world. Family members who are civilians are not taught that same degree of obedience. If they are told they need to move for their job, they often feel they can negotiate. They can discuss the situation with their boss and find alternative solutions. "I don't want to move; I can still do the job from my home office." The civilian world does not demand the same degree of conformity. It exists in a world of negotiations and compromises and individual identity. The military does not.

These contrasting worlds can and do cause familial stress. Military families earn the right to be called strong, resilient, and proud. But they also want us to be aware of their struggles. It is not because they feel we need to solve these problems for them; they may not want our sympathy, but they do want a degree of understanding. When we understand, we can support them. And when we support them, they are better prepared to maneuver through the various issues that they inevitably face.

When teachers understand military stressors, they can reach out and help the student who can no longer concentrate because mom just got deployed. When employers understand military stressors, they can be sensitive to their employee who is now, suddenly, both mom and dad in the family. When pastors understand military stressors, they can seek out families affected by the military in their church and community and give them needed spiritual advice and guidance.

As caring people in a complex world, we feel it is our duty to help others. And just like the good Samaritan, *who* we help and *when* we help is up to us. This book does not dictate how to behave; but it will clarify, inform, and educate you about what you can do for the military families in our midst.

Tips for Ministry

- Find out who in your congregation has a military connection. This can be done by hosting a military appreciation night and inviting all persons connected to the military to attend. And don't forget the connection goes beyond the spouse. It can and does include siblings, parents, grandparents, and neighbors.
- Start a military ministry in your church. It can be an official committee or it can be educating the entire congregation on how to be sensitive and caring to all of their neighbors, including those who are involved in the military. Many churches use sermons to highlight this sensitivity or train individual adult Sunday school classes.
- Ask military families what they need. And be specific when you offer a service. Don't say, "Call me if you need anything." Rather, say, "I am bringing over a meal on Friday unless I hear different from you."

CHAPTER TWO

The Soldier's Life: Why Is It So Hard to Come Home from War?

Endure hardship with us like a good soldier. . . . No one
serving as a soldier gets involved in civilian affairs—
he wants to please his commanding officer.
—2 Timothy 2:3-4 NIV

Some Soldiers Endure Hardship and Danger

Soldiering is a hard life for many in uniform. It involves the soldier and his or her family enduring many difficulties in pursuing this vocation well. It involves disengaging one-self from the multiplicity of civilian obligations and gaining a singular focus on the military mission. It also involves new ways of thinking, valuing, and acting to prepare one-self to engage in combat alongside fellow soldiers, sailors, airmen, and marines. A key part of being a good soldier means following orders and seeking to please your commander in achieving a mission of much greater importance than your own individual goals. It is a vocation that calls for self-sacrifice, courage, and the willingness, if necessary, to pay the ultimate price of laying down one's life in service to one's country.

I remember one day when, while serving as a Navy chaplain aboard a Pacific Fleet destroyer, I listened in on a "Welcome Aboard" speech by the ship's captain to a group of new sailors straight from boot camp reporting aboard ship. In his opening remarks, the captain said:

> I don't know why you joined the Navy. Maybe it was to get away from a girlfriend or parents in Philadelphia, maybe to learn a trade, or maybe just to see the world. But I just want you to know, the only reason you really are here is to fight and maybe die for your country! Our mission, if an enemy torpedo is heading toward the aircraft carrier we are defending, is for this ship to get between the aircraft carrier and the torpedo and take the torpedo hit and probably sink with all hands lost so the carrier can be saved. Now if you can embrace that mission and fit it in with all your other plans to get away from home, learn a trade, and see the world, we will get along just fine! If you have problems with that mission, you need to have a talk with the chaplain!

After those remarks, the captain dismissed the sailors. Later in the day a number of these new sailors found their way to my office on that ship, struggling to realign their civilian plans and personal goals with being called to a life of hardship and self-sacrifice for a bigger cause.

When military personnel leave the service, though they may not have liked the hardship and danger of military service, they will reflect with pride on the challenges they faced and overcame. Even in old age, they will remember with fondness the times they were tried and tested and found to measure up and carry out a tough job for their country. Many veterans will say, "It was the best time of my life" or will wistfully remember those years of *living life on the edge*.

One elderly paratrooper veteran from the 101st Airborne Division told his story of the night he parachuted into France in the Normandy Invasion, June 6, 1944:

> I was the best soldier I could have been that night that we jumped into Normandy. The buddies I was with were the

best and the bravest I've ever seen; I was lucky to be counted among them. We did God's work that night and the days that followed as we fought across Europe to defeat Hitler. I left my best self behind when I left the Army at the end of the war. Things have never quite been the same for me since. Everything else in my life after that night has been anti-climatic—just a footnote to that moment when I was really alive, young, and brave. I've never felt that way again!

That feeling of community and brotherhood among soldiers in the crucible of battle almost never can be duplicated in civilian life: this life of my brothers and sisters in arms is hard for soldiers to surrender when they come home from war. Few other occupations give people the feeling that they have their partner's back and that partner has theirs in a very intense situation.

Some Soldiers' Reasons for Joining the Military

Many people who have not served in the military ask, "Why would people want to join the armed forces and risk their lives in war? Why would anyone want to go in harm's way?" Yet every day across America, men and women line up at military recruiting offices and volunteer to serve their country in uniform. So what attracts these volunteers to military service?

Most soldiers were motivated to serve in the military long before they were of an age to join. Many soldiers grew up in homes of veterans, and they wanted to follow in the boots of a grandparent or parent, a brother or sister who served. These soldiers often heard the war stories of personal bravery shown by their dad or grandpa during the war. Many soldiers grew up with movies and television shows portraying war as a great adventure to be desired and an opportunity to become a hero. These childhood experiences, subtle as they seem at the time, influence young people to explore joining the armed forces.

Some veterans joined the armed forces due to a strong belief in the cause for which they were fighting. During World War II, many angrily volunteered to fight Japan after the Pearl Harbor attack. After 9/11 some joined the all-volunteer force to fight terrorists out of anger, but many more joined for employment and training opportunities, educational benefits, and a sense of purpose and meaning.

In World Wars I and II, as well as in the Korean and Vietnam wars, some veterans were involuntarily drafted into military service. These veterans became soldiers not out of choice but on threat of prison if they did not comply. Once in the service, however, most served honorably and with distinction and courage.

Through the years, soldiers, sailors, airmen, marines, and coast guard personnel also joined for the sheer adventure of the wartime experience. Every war America has fought since the Revolutionary War has included thrillseekers trying to avoid boredom in life.

Some veterans joined to escape life back home, where they dealt with family dysfunction, addictive behaviors, and abusive relationships. Some veterans over the years went into the service with the threat of a judge to "join the Army or go to jail." They were looking for a new start with a new "family," a band of brothers and sisters whom they could count on.

For still other recruits, going into the service was an escape from economic circumstances and lack of vocational and educational opportunities back home. These people were looking to the military for vocational training they could use later in civilian life (like air traffic control, aircraft maintenance, flying, electrical maintenance, or law enforcement). Opportunities for technical school or college education paid for by the military while in the service, or the promise of the GI Bill when leaving service, enticed many into the military.

In coming home from military service, these soldiers can find it hard to leave behind the discipline, structure, physical training, adventure, sense of camaraderie, and opportunity for improving themselves they found in the service, things that may be difficult to duplicate in civilian life.

All Soldiers Are Not Alike: Some Are Trained for Combat

Some soldiers are interested in the adventure of combat. They are trained in combat arms, learning to engage in close combat with the enemy with their advanced fighting skills. This group represents about 10 percent of active soldiers, with the remaining 90 percent in combat support roles and who are not regularly expected to directly engage the enemy. We can't assume that all soldiers have been in intense combat and are scarred for life with PTSD or war wounds. Most service personnel have been in the rear in combat support roles or were only occasionally exposed to serious danger in their service (this includes sailors on ships at sea, ground crews for aviation units of all services, and many supply personnel and administrative clerks).

Among Army soldiers and Marines who do go into a combat zone, more than 80 percent do just fine in adjusting to combat and later readjusting back home. The remainder of these war veterans struggle with readjustment issues, which we will address in more depth later.

Combat arms soldiers (infantry, armor, air defense, field artillery, aviation, engineers, and Special Forces) get qualified on a wide array of weapons, learning hand-to-hand combat techniques, advanced patrolling skills, and offensive and defensive tactics to survive on a battlefield. They build endurance and strength and learn to persevere in arduous battlefield conditions. In short, they get hardened to face the enemy in close combat and get trained to react instinctively to dangerous situations. If their lives or the lives of their battle buddies are being threatened, they are trained to reflexively kill the enemy before they are killed. After all, we want them to do whatever is necessary to survive and win the battles our country sends them to fight.

Combat soldiers often find it hard when leaving the service to trade in the action of combat arms missions for sitting behind a desk pushing a pencil for a business in civilian life.

All Soldiers Are Not Alike: Some Support Those in Combat

Some soldiers want to learn a trade that is transferable to the civilian world, so they train for combat support or combat service support roles. Combat support (intelligence, signal corps, military police, chemical warfare, etc.) and combat service support soldiers (finance, ordnance, quartermaster, transportation, medical service, etc.) may or may not be exposed to close combat. They work in supply warehouses, ordnance depots, and administrative offices. They may work in airfield flight line jobs or mechanical jobs or in a ship's engine room maintaining the propulsion system of a Navy cruiser. They face the stress of long hours of hard and often menial work to meet a mission requirement far from home. They may not get much glory or many medals for their service and may be derided by combat arms soldiers for their "in the rear with the beer" duty.

Yet, even here, these soldiers, when they return home, miss being part of making history in a cause that is bigger than themselves. They find it hard to adjust to working in, for example, civilian sales positions (after being on an important military mission), selling things that people don't really need so that they can earn money to buy things that they don't need. Sometimes merely living an everyday sort of life can trigger an existential search for deeper meaning and purpose for these veterans.

Some Other Important Differences

Besides differences in missions, soldiers are different in other ways. They come from different socioeconomic and academic backgrounds, so their starting place in the service may be very different. Soldiers with a college education are eligible for leadership and management positions as officers, while others with only a high school diploma, GED, or a little college qualify for enlisted positions in technical or combat fields. Some soldiers grew up in functional and nurturing families and others in more dysfunctional situations, either of which can impact their human relations skills as young adults in the military. Some are married and may have children, while others are single with fewer responsibilities for families back home.

We all know that there are differences in services, each with their own hardships and challenges. Life on an airbase or in an aviation unit is very different from being on a ship at sea or in the ground forces of the Army and Marine Corps. Deployment cycles may be shorter (60-90 days) and more frequent for Air Force personnel, somewhat more arduous for sailors (6-9 months), and very challenging for troops in the Army and Marines (in excess of a year away from home).

Thus, we should avoid thinking of military personnel or their families in a monolithic way, as if they were all alike. The differences in family upbringing, education, economics, and mental and spiritual health of soldiers prior to entering the service are significant in understanding these individuals. The mission that soldiers do and the roles they play in the military are also significant influences. Knowing a soldier's role as an officer or enlisted, whether on a combat or combat support mission, if on the first deployment or third deployment, or in the active forces or Reserves, all give us good information to help us understand and assist veterans.

Some Soldiers Are Stationed Far from a Combat Zone

A myth persists that all soldiers, sailors, airmen, marines, or coast guard personnel serve in combat. Many actually remain in the United States in support or training roles or are on overseas assignments far from the war, doing war deterrence or combat support missions.

Even of those who go into a combat zone, only a small percentage of Army soldiers actually wear on their chest a Combat Infantryman's Badge, Combat Action Badge, or Combat Medical Badge (or for Marine and Navy personnel, the Combat Action Ribbon), recognizing that individual has been in combat and fired upon by the enemy.

Thousands of sailors sailing the oceans have never had a shot fired at them in anger, while they ferry supplies to a war zone or patrol waters of the Atlantic or Pacific Oceans. Among naval service members only aviators, hospital personnel, special operations forces (SEALS), and chaplains generally get exposed directly to combat action today, because most combat is not at sea but in the air or on land where these sailors go.

Likewise, Air Force personnel are supporting supply missions and doing nuclear and conventional war deterrence missions from bases in the United States and in places like South Korea, Japan, Guam, and Germany, where no combat action is presently going on.

The Army and Marines are presently bearing the brunt of combat missions in the global war on terror. However, a number of Army combat brigades and their supporting forces are tied down in Korea and Europe, and a Marine division and air wing is located in Okinawa, Japan, to respond to conflicts in the Pacific region. Other Army divisions and brigades, not presently deployed, are garrisoned in the United States (including Alaska and Hawaii).

Some Soldiers Serve in the National Guard or Reserves

Some soldiers are invigorated by being full-time citizens and part-time soldiers. They like serving as "minutemen" on the home front, with occasional deployments overseas for national emergencies. For these part-time soldiers returning from long, full-time deployments, coming home represents the stress of trying to pick up the lives they left behind when they responded to the call to active duty as citizen soldiers. They are unlike their active duty regular force counterparts who, upon returning from a deployment, maintain their full-time work as regular soldiers and just go for more training or to a new duty station as the next step in their lifelong, full-time careers. National Guard soldiers and Reservists give up their full-time military jobs during demobilization. They go back to whatever civilian job they had before they mobilized, whether they liked that job or not, or whether it fits them now or not. Some of these veterans become unemployed or underemployed. Many soldiers in the National Guard and Reserves miss the pay, benefits, and security of active duty service when they demobilize.

Some Soldiers Enjoy Going on Deployments

There is a myth that most service personnel hate to go on deployments and dread the day they will have to go in harm's way. That is not true! Most single soldiers look forward to deployments. Even married soldiers may feel bad about leaving their families to go on a mission, but this is what they have trained for and generally they want to "do it for real." Pilots want to fly into action, sailors want to sail in harm's way, and solders and marines want to close with an enemy and defeat them.

Career-oriented service personnel often serve out of a sense of duty or calling and go on deployments to advance their military career. Like a police officer or firefighter who likes exciting and at times dangerous work, many professional soldiers take pride in their warrior skills and in using them to serve our country. "Soldiers want to fight," says retired Gen. Barry McCaffrey, who was the youngest and most decorated Army general when he retired in 1966. "That's why they signed up" (Stone, Conant, & Barry, 2009, p. 36).

When a soldier prepares for deployment, life can get a little crazy. Families are sad, angry, and grieving the departure of their soldier and generally feeling bad. Soldiers feel bad about parting also, but some honestly look forward to the mission and their chance to do what they have been trained to do. This often causes a disconnect between a soldier and his or her family and can lay seeds of anger and guilt that take root in the human heart for years to come. It is one of the invisible wounds of war that soldiers and family members carry.

Very quickly as a combat deployment begins, a soldier, sailor, airman, marine, or coast guard personnel begins to adapt to a new way of living, submitting to the discipline, core values, and habits of each service. They have moved into another world that is far from the civilian one they left. They quickly form into a team and begin to experience a dependence on and closeness with buddies whom they only recently met. They form a bond that is almost never replicated in civilian life.

Upon leaving the service or demobilizing from National Guard or Reserve active duty, these soldiers miss the adventure, the sense of purpose in their mission, and a deep feeling of camaraderie not easily found in the civilian sector. Many of these veterans, upon getting settled in the civilian world, soon want to go back into the service and volunteer for another deployment (if in the National Guard or Reserves), sometimes to the chagrin and dismay of their families.

Some Soldiers Learn Positive Things in the Service

Service personnel are challenged to be responsible and accountable for their actions. "No excuses, sir" is a common response of a soldier who screws up. They learn not to let one another down but carry their own weight and at times also carry the burden of a fellow soldier who is struggling. They stay alert and keep their weapons clean, ready to fight at a moment's notice to defend themselves and their battle buddies. They learn how to "ruck on," enduring hardship and deprivation of food and sleep and not falling out of formation and letting their buddies down. Courage and integrity are core values for those in uniform, and both are expected to be common virtues in the heat of battle. Disciplined living is a way of life for those in the service, from physical fitness to mental toughness. They learn how to show up on time, take orders to do a mission, and follow through and complete the task effectively and efficiently. They learn to perform their jobs well, often with little margin for error, with high standards for performance. They learn to look after one another and to live together unselfishly in a tight community that many have not experienced as civilians. They learn to control their emotions in stressful conditions, so as not to be overwhelmed with fear or anger in ways that prevent them from effectively leading—or following leaders—in combat.

What these veterans miss when they leave the service is a learning environment that constantly pushes them to stretch and grow to their full potential. It is an equalitarian culture where people are measured by their deeds rather than by their heritage, money, race, or religion—common discriminating factors in the civilian world. Large numbers of minorities join the service because they sense they will get an even break on the military parade ground that they will not get on Main Street back home.

Some Soldiers See Unforgettable Things in Battle

Some things soldiers see are just unforgettable. In battle, the experience of the pyrotechnics, blast noise, and sensation of air pressure changes from explosions nearby is shocking. Remember the movie *Apocalypse Now*, about the Vietnam War? Actor Robert Duvall, acting as LTC Bill Kilgore of the Army's 1st Air Cavalry Division, is leading a helicopter landing force into a contested landing zone. He watches jets drop napalm bombs, which explode in front of him and his men. He watches as flaming jellied gasoline washes over an enemy-occupied village and destroys it. Then the officer yells to one of his men:

Kilgore: Smell that? You smell that?
Lance: What?
Kilgore: Napalm, son. Nothing else in the world smells like that.
Kilgore: I love the smell of napalm in the morning. You know, one time we had a hill bombed, for 12 hours. When it was all over, I walked up. We didn't find one of 'em, not one stinkin' dink body. The smell—you know, that gasoline smell—the whole hill. Smelled like [*sniffing, pondering*] . . . victory. Someday this war's gonna end. [*suddenly walks off*]
(The Internet Database of Memorable Quotes for *Apocalypse Now*, 1979)

You see, hear, and smell things in war that you've never experienced anywhere in the civilian world! The sights of the machinery of war, from jets and helicopters roaring overhead, tanks rumbling by, screeches of artillery shells arching over your head and racing toward enemy targets, and soldiers or marines advancing on an objective in a mad-minute of weapons fire captures your fascination. It is all about being emotionally caught up in something bigger than yourself. It is focused aggression, throwing yourself into the breach to engage in battle and win a victory. This is the glory of war; the stuff you grow up dreaming about as a child, where you are the courageous one who becomes a hero in a decisive battle.

However, a combat-tested Marine veteran said as he watched such combat scenes: "It was a little like looking at pornography, arousing and exciting, yet somehow a little degrading, wanting to look, but also feeling a little ashamed to look at the sights of enemy soldiers being killed in front of your eyes."

Soldiers keep these images of battle in their minds long after guns have gone silent, something seldom shared and then only with battle buddies.

Then there is the dirty side of war. Soldiers see horrible things in battle, images that stick with them for the rest of their lives. While sailors can be on a ship or submarine and launch cruise missiles to targets far away, and Air Force pilots can fly Predator drones on missile-firing missions from thousands of miles away, soldiers and marines close with the enemy and do battle with them up close. They see dead bodies contorted in strange positions, watch beautiful towns flattened by artillery or bombs, and witness the pain and suffering of those wounded in action. They see limbs torn from bodies and combatants with sucking chest wounds struggling to breathe.

The carnage and the filth and the stench of war remain with veterans. Fighting in an infantry war is a dirty business, with soldiers going for several weeks without showering; they may have been pinned down by enemy fire and forced to relieve themselves in their pants; they may have been fighting and holed up for days with the stench of human waste, rotting bodies, and infected untreated wounds. It is a world where one rarely sleeps more than a couple of hours at a stretch and where the food is as warm or cold as the weather one is enduring. This is serious camping; only the "campers" can get killed doing it. It is a place filled with hours of boredom, punctuated by blindingly fearful moments when soldiers do not know if they will live to see another day. It is a place where freakish accidents happen and soldiers can begin to feel rather fatalistic.

A good litmus test of how much veterans have seen of combat is usually how much they talk about the experience: if they haven't seen much, they talk as though they have seen a lot; those who have seen much more than they ever wanted to see say little about their wartime experiences. These veterans may miss the spectacle of war, which can never be duplicated by any Fourth of July fireworks. They will not, however, miss the dirt and carnage of battle or the kind of life they had to lead to survive in combat. They can do without the bad dreams at night. But they will always remember and miss fellow soldiers with whom they were close.

Some Soldiers Do Things in War They Regret

One Vietnam War veteran recalled:

> I was assigned to drive a truck down the same road every day to get to a supply depot and bring supplies back to the base camp. Every day I drove a road that was filled with refugees walking alongside a road that was often mined and where snipers shot at my truck as I passed. The only way that I could daily run through this gauntlet was to get very drunk before I drove that road. Then I would just laugh as bullets punctured my windshield. I would slink down behind the steering wheel to provide as small a target as possible to the snipers, and I stepped on the gas. I could hardly see where I was driving. Sometimes I ran into refugees who got too close as I careened down that road. Now from time to time I think of those innocent people I think I ran over and I feel guilty about it.

Here is a soldier whose past deeds in war haunt him and who has no idea how to begin to make amends for his actions and experience grace and forgiveness. Many veterans who have done things they are not proud of in war struggle spiritually later in life because they feel guilty and unworthy of forgiveness for sins in their youth. They rarely darken the door of the church because they feel estranged from God. For some, it is impossible to right a wrong done in war, so they feel hopeless and are desperately in need of the ministry of absolution.

Some Soldiers Have Not Been Welcomed Home Properly

The history of how the American government has treated returning war veterans is a mixed bag of "tricks or treats." Our government has done good things for some veterans and has helped them come home. In other cases, the government agencies that some soldiers turned to for help with postwar problems have not provided the needed help.

One of the best moments of government intervention was the creation of the GI Bill in 1944, which helped returning veterans from World War II get education and training for new civilian jobs. That program created new opportunities for veterans to get on with their lives. The GI Bill was also cost effective. It made money for the government because of the increased taxes these newly educated and better-employed veterans paid.

> The 7.8 million veterans who took advantage of the WWII GI Bill ushered in an era of prosperity where for every tax dollar spent, the government received approximately $7 in return. The original GI Bill vastly expanded the middle class in America, improving the lives of veterans, and profoundly affected their families and all Americans. (Veterans Administration, *A Budget Report for 2009*, p. 17)

There were darker times in the treatment of veterans:

> Veterans all the way back to the Revolution, the War of 1812, the Mexican War, and World War I were refused

compensation for their service or it was delayed. Veterans from Mexico to Cuba were quarantined to die from tropical diseases; Korean prisoners of war were ignored and forgotten, Vietnam grunts were sometimes spit on and discriminated against. Veterans from Vietnam, Desert Storm, and from atomic experiments were refused treatment while the government denied their illnesses ever existed. (Taylor, 2007, p. 162)

The attitude of the public toward veterans returning from wars has also been mixed. There were enthusiastic welcome-home parades and celebrations for victorious veterans from World War II. Many Korean War and Vietnam War veterans, however, quietly limped home from war, one at a time, not in units, without fanfare or parades. And more than a few Vietnam vets were actually spit at by strangers when they returned home.

Quickly, however, after our wars were over and the parade bands quit playing, many returning veterans were simply forgotten by their communities. Their medical and mental health care was neglected or greatly underfunded by the government during administrations of both political parties. And veterans' organizations continue to lobby Congress for help, with limited success. Often, they end up doing most of the helping themselves, providing limited support for veterans in American Legion and Veterans of Foreign Wars posts in towns and cities across America.

Today, coming home for veterans is still scary. Vets wonder if they will ever find their place in life again. They wonder if it is just parades, yellow ribbons, and little more—just one big PR campaign for politicians, with little substance behind it. For many, especially in hard economic times, their active service component provided financial security unparalleled in the civilian community. When they come home, however, having survived the war, they fear upon demobilization that they may walk into a deadly economic ambush. Adjustments in getting back to civilian work, re-engaging with families, and finding meaning and purpose after serving in the military are big issues for modern-day veterans returning from war. For those with service-connected disabilities, painful rehabilitation and adjustments to living with disabilities is daunting.

Some Soldiers Come Home Ready to Get On with Life

There is a myth that the majority of those in uniform who return home after a war are broken people, struggling with PTSD (Post Traumatic Stress Disorder) or war wounds. That is not true. In reality, most of our veterans, at least 80 percent, are coming home prepared to quickly reengage with life at home and in the community and get on with a normal life.

Many veterans come back home after war having led soldiers in stressful battlefield conditions and become very responsible, courageous, innovative, disciplined, and resilient people who make great citizens in our communities. While away in the service, these veterans have learned to be very dependable people whose word is their bond. They will show up promptly for a 10 a.m. appointment, or five or ten minutes early, as they were taught to do in the military. They come home not wanting to waste time, entering college or technical schools with the help of the GI Bill, hoping to find a place in the workforce where they can make a decent living.

Some veterans come back having received excellent training in the service that is transferable to the civilian community: Many airline pilots, doctors, nurses, emergency medical technicians, computer technicians, auto and airline mechanics, police officers and firefighters, and nuclear plant operators all got their start in the military. Veterans who have been in leadership positions in the military return home and apply their abilities to inspire, lead, and manage organizations and people. Veterans become the next generation of employees and potential leaders in businesses, labor, education, government, and even church ministries. They are not "they," outsiders coming to live in our communities, but rather they are "us" returning to our communities from war.

Some Soldiers Need Just a Little Help in Coming Home

Coming home has never been easy for veterans. There have to be so many adjustments by both soldiers and their communities to make a veteran feel welcomed back home.

> Coming home from war is not going home from a day at the office, parking the car, checking the mail, and raiding the refrigerator. Living in mud makes them crude, facing death hardens them, and fear rattles their nerves; war leaves impressions that cannot be rubbed smooth, only concealed. After the first hugs and kisses, the first flush of reunion, suppressed anxieties come in disturbing and unpredictable ways. Then the trouble begins. (Taylor, 2007, p. 111)

During this time of adjustment veterans often report that they have lost their purpose and motivation in life. While in the service, they were the Sailor or Airman of the Quarter, the best marksman, or the top gun fighter pilot in the air wing. Now all of that is Confederate currency, ignored and nearly worthless in the civilian community.

Having given up for a time their place in the world of civilian work, these veterans need help to find new work. Many need education and retraining to replace jobs that have disappeared or which they have grown out of while away serving in the military. Many veterans, given the chance and with a little help, will find meaningful work and go on to live balanced lives. Others will struggle for a while with motivation to restart civilian life and may move from job to job for a time until they find something that grabs their interest and passion. Still others become workaholics, outwardly becoming great employees and good providers for their families, but they are never home. These need a gentle nudge to finish the journey, to come all the way home.

Veterans may need help in reuniting with spouses, children, and family after long absences. Changes have taken place in everyone's lives during the war, and everyone has to catch up with one another and establish new non-wartime rhythms in their lives.

These soldiers don't need a lot of help, just a little encouragement and patience from loved ones, some good job leads from friends, and direction for further schooling from community educators and VA representatives.

Some Soldiers Feel They've Lost Their Place in Life

One common issue for returning veterans is feeling they have lost their place in life. They try to find new work and also to figure out how they fit in with their family that has had its own routines while the soldier was gone. It's a feeling of not quite fitting in anymore and not knowing where to begin.

Friends have moved on to college and have new friends now; girlfriends or boyfriends have dropped them and moved on. Old jobs don't fit with their qualifications anymore, and veterans feel stuck right back where they started before deployment. Spouses may have changed and become more independent and distant; they may find it hard to recapture the spark of romance and love once felt. The veteran feels estranged from his or her own children and may try to make up for lost time with a lot of activity, but it doesn't work. The place where the vet once lived and dreamed of returning home to is just not where he or she wants to be anymore.

All of these feelings can lead to growth as veterans and their families tackle problems with patience and understanding. Everyone involved needs to let time be a friend and seek the support and counsel of veterans' assistance programs and community helpers in churches and in vocational and family counseling services.

Some Soldiers Need More Help than Others

Some soldiers don't want to go home or leave the service because they are struggling with Post Traumatic Stress Disorder (PTSD) or Traumatic Brain Injury (TBI) directly related to combat action. To be discharged from the wellness culture of the military, where fitness for duty is everything, is to lose many of the support systems and buddy support of comrades in arms. Coming home in this way is to leave the known world of the military to step into the strange world of the VA Medical System and community health care providers.

Some of these veterans come home and try to mask problems associated with these wounds of war. For the roughly 20 percent of soldiers who return with some degree of PTSD symptoms, this is not just a world of bad wartime dreams. PTSD involves daytime flashbacks of frightening images seen in combat, hyperarousal and hypervigilance to threats to themselves or others, poor concentration, and fear and withdrawal from crowds and other people. This is often accompanied by any one or several of a host of addictions, which are attempts to relieve mental pain. TBI involves memory loss that often looks like early Alzheimer's disease; the veteran forgets how to find the way home, or forgets the names of people who are closest to him or her. Attendant with these symptoms is often an ongoing struggle with depression that makes work and family living difficult.

Other veterans who may not have battle injuries still find adjusting to life back home difficult and painful. They find themselves spiraling into depression, chemical abuse, gambling, pornography, sexual addictions, risk-taking behavior, anger, and abusive behavior. Usually these demons are legion, not just a single issue, pulling these veterans quickly down into the quicksand of suicidal or violent and abusive behavior. All too frequently these behaviors lead to incarceration, injury, or death.

In these cases, serious interventions are necessary by family members, church leaders, mental health professionals, employers, law enforcement, judicial systems, or health care providers. Rarely do these veterans "put themselves on report," since they often delude themselves about their mental status and minimize their problems. By the time these adjustment issues are identified and their origin is recognized, it is too late. The stigma preventing veterans from seeking mental health services is very strong, after serving in a "ruck on" and "embrace the suck" military culture. Intertwine these cultural values of enduring pain with the denial mechanisms common in addictive behavior, and one can easily see others in the community needing to intervene for the veteran as he or she sinks into chronic addictive behavior. Anyone wanting to help needs a few phone numbers on speed dial to reach veterans' service or community social service contacts who can help triage the situation and direct helpers toward necessary resources to help veterans in trouble.

A Few Concluding Thoughts

Our wish for our returning veterans is that, ten years from now, when they have a reunion of their unit, they will show up wearing fishing hats and baseball caps of their favorite teams. We do not want to see any of them wearing faded Army caps or old worn-out uniforms from the Iraq or Afghanistan War (like so many Vietnam War vets did after that war), indicating they are still living in the past. We want our soldiers to make it all the way home and reintegrate back into our communities to become productive citizens and leaders of tomorrow.

We want to enlist the help of people of faith, to assist our troops to make the transition from military life to life on Main Street. It is our hope that, with the help of the faith community, many of our troops will find our churches safe and welcoming places to which to come home and receive ministry, inspiring them, in turn, to become a part of that ministry reaching out to others in need in our communities. Let's welcome our troops home—all the way home!

Tips for Ministry

- Don't view all service personnel and their families as the same: value their differences and their varied experiences as you seek to minister to them and recruit them for church ministries.
- Most service personnel and their families take great pride in their service and sacrifice: acknowledge their service and appreciate their sacrifices without getting into politics over national policy, which they have no control over while in service. They follow the orders of our elected officials and the commander in chief!
- Be sensitive to soldiers, sailors, marines, airmen, and coast guard personnel who have been wounded physically, mentally, or spiritually in war: Educate congregational care teams on community and veteran resources to help returning service personnel get the help they need to heal from the wounds of war and to reintegrate back into our communities.
- Ask veterans what they did during the war. Were they involved in combat or were they in a supporting role? This will help you know what kind

of challenges they have faced so that you can better serve them, pointing them to places where they can get help for their needs.

- Be a good neighbor and welcome our soldiers all the way home: help them with vocational and personal adjustments in rejoining our communities and assist them in recovering spiritually within the community of faith.

CHAPTER THREE

Military Family Challenges: Living in a Warrior Culture

For everything there is a season, and a time for every matter under heaven: A time to kill, and a time to heal; a time to break down, and a time to build up; a time to weep, and a time to laugh; a time to mourn, and a time to dance. —Ecclesiastes 3:1, 3-4

The late ABC radio news commentator Paul Harvey was a great storyteller. He always began his broadcast telling some news story, and then he paused halfway through the story in cliff-hanging fashion and went to a commercial. When he came back on the air after the advertisement, Paul Harvey would say, "and now for the rest of the story."

Military deployments are somewhat like a story. In the beginning there is a time of sadness and parting, followed by a long parenthesis (similar to a commercial), the absence during the deployment, and then telling the rest of the story of a joyful homecoming and celebration. It is a story of a roller coaster ride filled with emotions: sadness, anger, and fear as the ride begins; twists and turns of what sometimes seems a never-ending ride in the middle; joy, relief, and earned confidence at the end. The military family's story is similar to this.

The Beginning of the Story

It all started on a blustery morning, the wind whipping mercilessly across the western prairie town. The National Guard unit was preparing to leave for a combat deployment to Iraq. The formation to board the airport-bound buses had not been called yet, so many couples and family members clustered together one last time to tearfully hug a soldier. Off to the side of the armory, one family gathered in a close circle, and those within earshot could hear the patriarch of the family praying for God's protection for their teenaged soldier. Some soldiers were leaning against the wall outside the armory, standing alone, quietly smoking one last cigarette. Having been hugged goodbye and dropped off earlier by a spouse, parent, or friend, they avoided this last-minute scene. The soldiers couldn't help thinking this deployment could very well put them in a place where they might take an enemy combatant's life—"a time to kill."

Soon the formation was called, and the soldiers lined up at attention and heard the orders of the commanding officer to prepare to go to war then filed onto buses already loaded with their baggage. The doors were shut and the engine revved as the bus pulled away from the armory, with families and friends tearfully waving goodbye to their soldier going to war. As the bus turned the corner and disappeared from sight, many family members hugged one another, some cried, and still others stoically walked quietly to their cars to make the drive home. For families, it was a time to try to face the absence of their soldier for another year or longer—"a time to weep and mourn."

The Middle of the Story

The middle of the deployment for a military family is like a big parenthesis in life, where time is suspended. They are at the armory again, participating in monthly Family Readiness Group (FRG) support meetings for spouses and parents, talking about the challenges of another military deployment, and learning coping strategies to deal with the absence of their loved one. These are the people who can really understand and appreciate how difficult deployments can be.

It is "a time to build up" and form supportive relationships to keep going during a long deployment. Family members talk about the challenges of single parenting, tell about kids' rebellious attitudes or not doing well in school, and share concerns about feeling isolated, lonely, and perhaps unsafe. Others comment on the financial issues they face while their spouse is gone. Some spouses have had to limit work hours or quit work altogether to care for the family as a single parent. Some National Guard and Reserve members' families live on less because their soldiers left financially rewarding civilian jobs to serve. A soldier's mother talks about trying to manage her anxiety as she pictures her son driving trucks down roads embedded with IEDs (improvised explosive devices) that could injure or kill him. She says she is a CNN junkie and is unable to tear herself away from the TV, where she waits for any scrap of news from Iraq. But she has other family members who need her, and she is determined to take care of herself and stay strong for them.

Now, after a Long Deployment—We Hear the Rest of the Story

Twenty-two months later, the same families find themselves back at the armory eagerly awaiting the arrival of their loved ones back from the war. There are American flags and yellow ribbons flying in the warm July breeze and a band is playing patriotic numbers. Soon a state patrol car with emergency lights flashing turns the corner toward the armory, leading a column of buses full of soldiers coming home. A cheer goes up, and the band strikes up a rousing version of "The Army Goes Rolling Along."

What follows is a blur for the families: straining for the first sight of their loved one getting off the bus; watching the formation and dismissal of the troops; and then running, along with hundreds of other family and friends, toward their soldiers and finally embracing and kissing them. It is a great time, filled with laughter and excitement as soldiers come home from war and reunite with family and friends—"a time to laugh and dance."

Our story does indeed have a beginning, middle, and end. But it has more. Most endings to stories are just that, the end. But the military story goes beyond the end. The yellow ribbons that welcome home a soldier are not the end but rather the beginning. It is the beginning of reintegrating a soldier back into his home and community. It is the beginning for many families of trying to re-establish themselves based on the changes all have made during the deployment cycle. Our story does indeed go beyond the yellow ribbons.

Military Families among Us: Historical Changes

Years ago, it was commonly heard in the service, "If the Army (Navy-Air Force-Marines-Coast Guard) wanted you to have a family, they would have issued you one!" When the Japanese struck Pearl Harbor in 1941, the Army and Navy were mostly made up of single personnel waiting out the Great Depression who joined up to "see the world." Only more senior officers and NCOs (noncommissioned officers) were paid enough to support a family. Today, "more than half the military population is married (54%) and 47% of the force have children. In addition, 70% of military spouses are employed" (*Military Human Resources*

Strategic Plan, Office of the Under Secretary of Defense for Personnel and Readiness, August 2002).

With family and military obligations vying for the attention of the soldier in much more dramatic ways than his or her civilian counterpart, the situation is primed for increased stress and tension at home and at work. Instead of being single-minded on the military mission like service personnel in 1941, today those in uniform who are married find they have to have a dual focus on the war front and on the home front. The viability of these marriages depends on the strength of a couple's relationship and good communication skills before joining the service—and the ability to maintain that relationship and those communication skills.

Military families are often proud, independent, and resilient. They put up flags in their driveways, put yellow ribbon stickers on their cars, and speak up for military rights. In a *USA Today* May 21, 2009 Memorial Day weekend article entitled "More than a Long Weekend," Kathy Roth-Douquet writes that, in spite of many challenges to family life, the majority of military families are proud of the service they render to their country.

Casey Spurr's Navy husband has had three deployments in the past five years, missing half of his four-year-old son's life. But she says, despite the sacrifice, it's "the honor of a lifetime" to be part of a military family. What animates these families is what John McCain called "a cause greater than self-interest." Military families want to be remembered, and not just because they want sympathy or help. They believe there is a benefit that comes from being part of a larger endeavor, and they don't want the larger society to miss out on that either.

Despite this display of support and congeniality, each military family harbors its own set of challenges and issues. Many of these issues are exacerbated during the deployment cycle: loneliness, isolation, single parenting, financial stress, poor communication, and fear.

Deployment Cycles

Pre-deployment

Families can have a considerably long notice about an upcoming deployment. It is not uncommon for a family to know almost one year in advance. Others may have only a few weeks' notice. Pre-deployment is a time of preparation. The family of the deployed soldier must accept that he or she will be leaving. There are also practical implications, such as who will take care of my son's home while he is deployed? How will I know what the baby wants when my wife is thousands of miles away? The future becomes cloudy with the unknown. Here is the way one soldier's wife described that pre-deployment period:

> Johnny knew almost one year out before he deployed with his unit. One year was too long. I kept trying to make plans into the future with vacations, reunions, etc. and would have to correct myself. I would say things like, "Won't it be nice for us to go out East for my niece's wedding." And then I would have to stop. He wasn't going to be home, and I could not include him in my plans.

There are three main dimensions identified for family readiness during this stage. They are financial readiness, readiness related to household responsibilities, and emotional or mental readiness. Research indicates that success in preparing for deployment depends on maturity, quality of marriage, and number of previous deployments. Families who have been married longer do better overall in preparing for deployments. Longer length of marriage correlates to a higher maturity level (RAND, National Defenses Research Institute, 2008). Families who have had a longer history together have had experience in dealing with a variety of issues, including previous deployments.

Maturity often comes with age. The average age of service members is mid-twenties. They have often been married for only four or five years and usually have one or two children. Although this is significant, it is still quite young in terms of the maturity and wisdom that come from life experiences. For many soldiers and their families, deployment is a test. Many men and women struggle with fidelity to their spouse. Will my husband in Iraq be faithful to me? Will my wife back home be faithful to me? For many couples, the question of infidelity looms large in their minds. Mature couples who have many years together have usually learned to trust each other. Although they too may have issues regarding fidelity, they have years of life experience and a track record to validate whether this may be an issue.

The pre-deployment stage is often filled with conflicting emotions. The parents of a single soldier may be very proud of their daughter's upcoming service to her country. But while praising her service, they may also be questioning the role they may now have to assume. More than 40 percent of our military personnel are single soldiers, marines, airmen, sailors, and coast guard personnel (RAND, National Defense Research Institute, 2008). Many of these service members have to rely on their parents to "take care of things" while they are gone.

> My daughter was notified three weeks before she deployed. What a whirlwind of issues we had to confront, both legal and emotional. Who would take care of her house? Could she get out of her cell phone lease? What legal papers did we need to sign? Would she be OK? How would we stay in touch? We hardly had time to breathe, let alone confront these issues. We were exhausted even before she left and we still had so much to finish.

Married couples often state that tension during the pre-deployment stage only intensifies as the deployment date looms closer and closer. Many couples and parents of single soldiers report that they are surprised at how much they disagree and fight during the weeks prior to deployment. It is as if they need to start letting go of one another even before the soldier leaves.

Many people are surprised by this intense tension. Most people assume that they will spend their last weeks together in some type of "preparation bliss." As the departure time draws near, there is often "silence" about potential fears, including injury or death. Both family and soldier seem to adhere to the military's directive of "suck it up and drive on." The soldier may feel he or she needs to "stay strong" and leave without any emotional tangles, pretending that he or she is actually glad to be leaving his or her family. The family may want to begin thinking of their soldiers in a less-than-favorable light so that they can send them away with the idea of being glad they are gone. This adds to the confusion and chaos that accompanies the deployment. When the soldier has departed, there is often intense guilt and anger. Many family members wish they had memories of a "sweet send-off," and many soldiers feel they did not say goodbye in a loving and caring way. Because they will not be together for a long time, they often use the last few weeks as the memory of their soldier they hang on to. But this memory is usually not the proper one, since it includes so much of the tension and unrest prior to deployment.

Deployment

Deployments can last from one to twenty-four months. Most deployments are in countries far from home. Some soldiers have jobs in which they face constant danger. Other soldiers are assigned jobs where they don't leave their bases, and instead of safety issues, there are overwhelming issues of boredom.

After a loved one has left, the remaining family members must adjust to having him or her gone. The adjustment to this reality takes time. Many spouses and parents of deployed soldiers will state that the first few weeks are a time of acceptance and then planning. Families with children, especially young children, often work on routines. They develop reliable schedules to help them ease into being a single parent through deployment.

Twenty-five percent of surveyed military families state that the beginning of the deployment is the most difficult. This was followed by 29 percent that consider the middle part the most difficult. Eighteen percent say departure is the most difficult. Fourteen percent say notification of an impending deployment is the hardest, while 8 percent say that the end of the deployment is the hardest (*National Military Family Association Survey*, 2005). Many soldiers return home midway through their deployment for rest and recreation (R and R). This can be a very stressful time for military families. After several months of being without their soldier, the family has often gotten into a new routine and may state that "although it is hard, we are doing OK." Then they get the news that their soldier can return home for two weeks. Initially this seems like an answer to prayer. The children get to see their dad; married couples get to reunite. But then the questions form. Do we want to see him for two weeks only to let him go again? Parents of young children especially worry that schedules and routines that have helped them manage will be ignored. Is it worth the emotional and physical disruptions to be together for such a short time only to start all over again? Families wrestle with this question and find there are no easy answers.

Families surveyed for a recent study report that they rely on three main informal supports to help them during deployment. The first line of informal support is usually family members. More than 57 percent of interviewed spouses state that it is their families they rely on the most. Family includes siblings, parents, and in-laws. About a third of spouses cite their local religious organization as their second line of support. Religious support usually means their church. The third line of support is friends and neighbors. Less than 10 percent of the interviewed spouses indicate Red Cross, other military spouses, or the Internet as a source of support (RAND, National Defense Research Institute, 2008). When it comes right down to it, family members recognize that they will have to rely on their own strength and resilience to help them most during deployment. "Soon after Tom left I was hit with the reality that it was now 'all up to me.' If the basement flooded or if the car broke down or if I needed to make a quick decision, it was all up to me. I was alone. And it scared me."

When military spouses were asked, "What is the greatest challenge for your family during deployment?" 71 percent answered, "Concern for my soldier's safety" (*National Military Family Association Survey*, 2005). This high percentage does not fit in with the reality of most soldiers' experience, even during wartime. The majority of soldiers do not get in harm's way. They are in supportive roles and their mission is not combat or convoy driving but rather filling out forms, ordering supplies, or working in telecommunication. Nevertheless, military families are very concerned about their loved one's safety and feel it acutely on a daily basis.

When a soldier is killed in action, it is the military's duty to inform the spouse or parent that their loved one has been killed. This is done in the daytime by a Casualty Affairs Officer and a chaplain. They come together to the house in their dress uniforms to notify a family of the death of the soldier. They usually do not call prior to coming.

> I never, ever got used to the doorbell ringing during the middle of the day. Ever. One time I had just put the baby down for his afternoon nap when the doorbell rang. I was not expecting anyone. My heart seemed to stop. I felt paralyzed. I forced my shaking legs to walk into the entry

way to answer the door. I mentally braced myself for uniformed officers to be there. I opened the door to see a mailman holding a package. I almost burst into tears from both my anxiety and joy.

Many military families learn how to cope as a single parent or as the parent of a deployed soldier. Recent Department of Defense research states, "In general, the majority of the families coped well or very well, as reported by sixty-three percent of the spouses" (RAND, National Defense Research Institute, 2008). This research also indicated that families who coped the best had a higher pay grade, older children, and a longer history in the community where they lived.

Post-deployment

Excitement about a soldier's return is often clouded with doubts. Will my dad still love me? Will my son have changed? What if my wife doesn't like how I raised the kids while she was gone?

Soldiers are also conflicted about reuniting with their family. Will I fit back into my home life? Will I still have a role? Will the kids know who I am? Does my spouse still love me?

Initially most soldiers have a "honeymoon" period that may last from several days to several months. This honeymoon is the "Welcome Home" phase. There are often parties and activities that bring the soldier and his or her family and friends together. The soldier is able to eat foods that he has craved for many months. He can sleep in his bed and reunite with the children. But the newness and excitement of being home often are soon overwhelmed by readjustment problems.

Soldiers report that returning home is much more difficult and confusing than anticipated. While deployed, soldiers were told what to wear, what to eat, and what to do for their mission each day. Once home, the soldier is no longer told what to wear, eat, or do. And despite most people's preference for choice, a soldier may discover that having unlimited choices can make life complicated.

A soldier who recently returned home may not know what her five-year-old son wants or needs. Balancing the checkbook may seem overwhelming. Choosing what to wear each day may seem like an insurmountable task. Many soldiers report that they initially have difficulty making even small decisions:

> I was amazed at how little I could think when I first got home. The second day home my mother called me and asked me what she should bring over for dinner. I had no idea. She gave me several choices and I still could not choose. Did I want spaghetti or pizza? Did I want garlic bread or breadsticks? These were all simple choices, and yet I was not used to choosing. I finally had to tell her she could pick and that it did not matter to me.

Spouses often struggle in letting a soldier back into the family routine. He or she has had to learn how to manage without the soldier. And some learn to manage very well. Routines are set and schedules are followed. The returning soldier may seem to "be in the way." And since the soldier may have difficulty making choices, he may simply get out of the way and let the spouse stay in charge. This may work for a while, until the spouse in charge remembers that she does have another adult in the house and that she needs help.

> I knew that Jason would have some readjustments after he got home. I was very patient at first. I let him sleep in and did not mind when he was quiet and needed time alone. I understood. I kept to my usual routine, but it was hard not having him help me. One day, about three weeks after he came home from Iraq, I reached my tolerance level and lost patience. The kids were all irritable

and fighting with one another. The dog got out and had to be found. I needed to start dinner. And then my husband came up from the basement where he had been watching television. He saw the chaos, shrugged, and walked into our bedroom. "Come back," I yelled, "I need help." He walked back in with a confused look on his face. "Help?" he repeated. "What kind of help?"

Despite the struggles faced during the post-deployment cycle, the majority of soldiers feel that they have been able to readjust successfully after being home for approximately one year. Most families learn to cope with a "new normal." They have changed and their soldier has changed. Once they have accepted that things are different, they can build on the strengths learned while apart. However, there is always a nagging and disturbing question for most military families: will my soldier deploy again?

Re-deployment

Fear of re-deployment can pose a barrier to readjustment. Many families are afraid to "get too close again" because he or she will leave again anyway. This threat of being separated can cause many physical and emotional barriers. This is not an idle fear. Since September 11, 2001, there have been approximately 1.5 million American troops deployed. One-third of them have served at least two tours in a combat zone. More than 70,000 of them have been deployed three times and at least 20,000 troops have been deployed as many as five times (*A Preliminary Report of the Psychological Needs of the US Military Service Members and Their Families*, TF Report, 2006). Most often, the military dictates to the soldier when he or she will be deployed. However, there are always soldiers willing and wanting to return. The reasons to re-deploy are varied and complex. Some soldiers go back for the adventure or to "finish a job." Others enjoy the increase in pay, and yet others want to return to the life they know in deployment. These soldiers may yearn to be in a routine that is predictable and relatively simple.

Military families face a variety of challenges after the soldier returns home. But the number one listed challenge is "concern of deploying/mobilizing again." Some 43 percent of military families call this their number one issue (*National Military Family Association Survey*, 2005).

> I was so glad when Jenny returned from Iraq. Our boys, four and two, could not seem to get enough of their mom. It seemed so right to have us all in the living room laughing and being silly. I would be involved in the fun when a nagging thought would find its way into my brain. "What if Jenny deploys again?" And then the moment would change and I would feel more sad than silly. I could feel myself pull away a bit. If she left we would have to start all over. And I am not sure I could face another deployment.

Most humans want to protect themselves from emotional pain. They try to circumvent the pain by becoming numb or immune to it. Military families seem to reserve the right to fully accept the soldier back into their lives. They don't want to get "too comfortable" or "too happy," because it could all change in six months.

Married to the Military

Triangulated Relationships

Soldiers, marines, sailors, airmen, and coast guard personnel join the military for a variety of reasons. But no matter what the initial reason for joining, many service members become acculturated into their particular branch and are fiercely loyal. They form an allegiance with fellow soldiers and begin to relate to them as a family. There is a stringent hierarchy of authority. Soldiers have limited choices and must follow orders. When military orders conflict with family plans, the family's wishes almost always take a back seat.

Military spouses are often discouraged and disheartened to realize that usually the military comes first. This is one of the features of being married to a soldier that is far less prevalent in marriages to civilians engaged in other careers. Spouses of soldiers will sometimes become angry or frustrated and issue an ultimatum: "It is me or the military." This puts the soldier, who wants to please the spouse, in a no-win situation. If the soldier pleases the spouse in this situation, they face the ire of the military disciplinary system, and if they please the military, they face the anger of a spouse.

> I remember our tenth wedding anniversary so clearly. I had made reservations at a fancy restaurant overlooking the ocean in San Diego. I had found a sitter for our three young daughters and I had purchased a very expensive dress. I had asked Larry weeks ahead of time if we could have that night together. He assured me he would be home. Imagine my shock and anger when Larry called two hours prior to our date and said he would not be able to come home. His commander needed him for the evening and it might run very late.

Military service has always been hard on the marriages of soldiers and their spouses. Stacy Bannerman, in her article "Broken Military Marriages: Another Casualty of War" written early in 2009 for AlterNet.org, stated, "More than 13,000 military marriages ended last year." Her explanation is that military families are under incredible pressures, especially those in branches of the armed services who are currently deployed over and over again. She cites a study published in the *Armed Forces and Society* that revealed that male combat veterans were 62 percent more likely than civilian males to have at least one failed marriage. Factors contributing to divorce included being apart for long periods of time, poor communication skills, isolation from social networks, and financial issues.

Those in the field of mental health recognize that emotional triangles are unhealthy and destructive to relationships. Soldiers and their spouses, however, must learn to live within a relational triangle composed of husband, wife, and military. All three are dependent on one another: The military mission cannot succeed if large numbers of soldiers leave the service to accommodate spouses' wishes for them to leave. Meanwhile, the civilian spouse and family depend on the soldier's military income for their support. Finally, the soldiers, particularly those who are parents, depend upon their spouses to keep the family and home functioning while they are away from home.

For the military-family triangular relationship to succeed, it must be acknowledged and nurtured by all parties involved. To have a good, functional marriage in the military requires a couple to make many personal accommodations for the sake of the military mission. If a couple cannot embrace the mission and challenges of military life as a team, they will have a difficult time in their marriage while in the military.

A sailor, incarcerated in the Navy brig in San Diego, told a story that illustrated this triangulated relationship:

> I came home a week before a WESTPAC (the western Pacific Ocean) deployment to an angry wife. She expected me to go tell the ship captain that I would not be going "because my wife needs me at home." I told her "there's no way I could do that. I could be in such trouble." She insisted, "Make a choice. It's me or the ship. We can run away together, someplace where the Navy can't find us." I chose her and went UA (unauthorized absence). We went to her mom's cabin in Colorado. Life was pretty good for nine months, until I got stopped

speeding. There was an outstanding warrant for my arrest, and they dragged me back here to court-martial me for desertion. Now my wife has filed divorce papers because she wants nothing to do with me. She says I brought all kinds of pain into her life because of the Navy.

It is a "hanged if you do, hanged if you don't" situation for that sailor, caught between the military and a non-military spouse. Couples often cope by means of the military member asking their partner to endure tough times, promising better times will come with the next assignment. With limited power to influence assignments, the soldier often finds the promise hard to fulfill. This leads to further marital conflict and a lack of trust on the part of the spouse and family regarding promises of a better future.

Broken Promises

Sometimes at the last minute the military will insist that a service member change his or her personal plans to fulfill a military commitment, resulting in disappointment and anger in the family. Families learn to be wary about planning for any special occasions because the military superior can squash those plans with a last-minute assignment. If this unpredictability is repeated again and again in a soldier's family, they become less and less resilient in handling the next disappointment.

Military families are often unable to plan or control their own lives. After awhile, many family members adopt the "don't talk, don't trust, don't feel" rules of behavior in a dysfunctional family. Soldiers in these families feel powerless to make and keep promises, so they stop making plans and just take a fatalistic view of life. Family members don't feel safe to complain about issues openly since they can jeopardize the soldier's career. They assume the military will disappoint them again and feelings are shut down. It can feel similar to life in an alcoholic family, where promises are made and then broken. Many military families quit making plans because, using a card game metaphor, those plans get trumped so often by the military that it destroys the very concept of promise-making and promise-keeping.

The families of soldiers never hold a strong suit of cards to win a hand against the military's hand in any really important "game." The powerlessness the spouses often feel leads to chronic depression, triangulation, and a culture of broken promises. The spouse of a soldier either becomes sadly resigned to repeatedly play a losing power game or the spouse can take control. The spouse can quit the game altogether and divorce the soldier or persuade the soldier to leave the military. One other option is to live a parallel life, with one's own career and separate interests, disengaged as much as possible from their spouse's military career.

This triangulation and culture of broken promises are keys to understanding chronic relational problems in military families. These relational problems can span generations long after uniforms are packed away. The legacy of anger and guilt in military families is one of the great hidden wounds of war that is rarely recognized or adequately mourned.

Children Face Their Own Struggles

Of the troops deployed since 9/11, roughly 890,000 have been parents ("Children of Conflict," Jessica Ramirez, *Newsweek* Magazine, June 15, 2009). Having a primary parent deployed for an extended length of time takes a toll on children. Children of all ages in military families face stressors, grief, and anxiety that are usually not faced by their civilian counterparts. How children adapt to the deployment cycle is influenced in part by the age of the child.

Babies and toddlers have limited reasoning and conceptualization skills. But even the youngest child can react to the emotions he or she feels in the home. When a parent deploys, the remaining parent often feels overwhelmed and sad, especially in the beginning stage of the deployment. The baby or toddler may need extra cuddling and support at the time his or her parent is least able to give it.

> Julia was always such a happy baby. And then Todd deployed. I know Julia did not know her dad was in Afghanistan, and yet it seemed that she started crying inconsolably the day he left. She seemed to startle more easily and whimpered when I tried to set her down. I was often unsure of what she needed, and I seemed to have so little to give her. Often we were crying at the same time!

Preschoolers are at an age where they begin to understand that there is a change in the family. They miss their deployed parent and react strongly to his or her absence. They have limited language skills and will often act out their anxiety and frustrations. The parent at home may notice changes in their child's temperament and attribute it in part to the deployment. Children in this stage of childhood may also feel their sense of safety challenged. They may need to have lights on in their rooms or insist on sleeping at night with their parents so they can feel secure.

Children in this stage may also think that their parents left for a deployment because of something they did. They may ask themselves, "What did I do that was so bad that Mom left for Iraq?" If they feel they did something wrong, they may also decide that if they are "good enough" they can bring their missing parent back home. The non-deployed parent may notice his or her child start to take on perfectionistic traits. The formerly messy child may start picking up all of his toys. Their normally demanding daughter may quit asking for things and do whatever she is asked to do. Initially having an obedient child may seem a relief. But then it becomes evident that trying to be perfect can be overwhelming for a child, and he or she starts acting more robotic than childlike.

Younger elementary-age children are very aware of the deployment and are often very sad about it. They may not feel as though they fit in at school with the other children and may withdraw. It is not uncommon during this stage for a child with a deployed parent to stick close to home. He or she may not want to venture too far in case something were to happen to the remaining parent. They want the missing parent to return home but have no control over making that happen.

Older elementary and middle school age children can become very vocal about the deployment. This stage of childhood often centers on issues of fairness. "That's not fair" is heard again and again. Children in this stage want to fit in. They don't want to be perceived as different, since different is often interpreted as "weird." Many children feel angry that all of their friends seem to have accessible parents, while he or she has one parent thousands of miles away in a combat zone.

This stage also can trigger the child's view of the deployed parent as the "preferred parent." If a child asks to do something and her at-home parent says "no," then she may counter with, "Dad would let me do it if he was home." This puts the at-home parent in a difficult situation. She wants to remain firm with her answer but is not always clear about what the deployed parent would say. She also may have limited energy to argue and may give in to the child's demands just to keep peace in the family.

> I hated when Lucy used to play the "but Dad would let me" routine. She usually did it on Friday nights when she would go to a friend's house. When she left I would tell her that there were to be no sleepovers that night. Inevitably the phone would ring just before I was to pick her up. "Mom," she would say, "is it OK if I sleep

over at Kelsey's house?" Of course, I would tell her no. She would ask again in a more whiny voice. Back and forth we would go, and then finally in a venomous voice she would say, "I know Dad would let me if he was home."

The teenage years are fraught with ragged emotions that keep teens seesawing between being a child and becoming an adult. This push-pull phenomenon often results in confusion and chaos. One day a teen may seem carefree and confident, followed by a day filled with anxiety.

When a parent deploys, the parent at home often feels overwhelmed. How can she possibly take care of four children, work during the day, and find time to be both the mother and the father? A parent of a teenager may find herself relying more and more on the teenager to fulfill the role of the other parent. She may ask her son to drive the younger children to baseball or to dance. Or, because she needs to go to work, she may ask her daughter to prepare the meals or stay home from school to help care for a younger child who is sick.

Some teenagers relish the idea of being a "mini-parent." They like the added responsibilities because it gives them a sense of purpose. Others like the new responsibility because they know that with responsibilities often come privileges. They may have access to a car, or perhaps they are allowed to stay out later because they have been "such a help at home."

Other teenagers resent the fact their mom or dad is deployed. They dislike the idea that they are forced into helping at home. They may have strong opinions of the military and feel that their deployed parent is wrong and that all wars are immoral. Teenagers are trying on new identities, and these may be in direct opposition to what their parent feels. This conflict adds to the strain and stressors already found in the home of a deployed soldier.

The Story Continues

Going beyond the yellow ribbon means helping soldiers and their families during the entire deployment cycle and beyond. Too often we assume that since the soldier is home, all must be well. Wasn't their departure the cause of the problems in the first place? But, as noted, many issues start when the soldier arrives home. Churches are in a unique position to help families beyond the yellow ribbon. They are a body of believers who have been taught to help others and to show kindness and compassion to all they encounter. As the story continues we can become part of it.

Tips for Ministry

- Military families want churches to know they have unique needs but also want churches to know that they are basically like everyone else.
- Many military families would benefit from a church member "mentor" who could provide ongoing support such as taking their children to a ball game or shovelling the snow or cutting the grass. Some of these mentors have come from men's and women's groups as well; others were recruited directly through the church newsletter or weekly bulletin. Usually a coordinator oversees this mentorship and helps assign church volunteers to identified families.
- Military children often love to talk about the service their parent is providing to the country. Give them opportunities to share their stories. Have the children bring in a map or poster of where their parent is deployed. Let them share ideas of what their parent may need. The children can collect pictures and letters made by the Sunday school

class or they can send the parent phone cards the other children have collected.

- Military families need support during every stage of deployment. Some tips for each stage:

1. Pre-deployment: Start working on ideas for helping families who will be affected by impending deployment. Put together volunteer ideas. Work with the military family to discover what they might need. Make sure they know who you are and what you can do to help prior to the start of the deployment.
2. Deployment: Keep in touch with the family. Call often and ask how it is going. Offer help with specific times or services. Don't just assume they will call you if they need something. Most likely they will not directly ask for help. Remember, issues and needs may change over time.
3. Post-deployment: Stay connected with the family. Now that the dad or mom is back, the family may not need the same kinds of help, but they also don't want to be forgotten. Bring them into the circle of caring members. Invite the soldier to tell his or her story. Keep the military connection alive.

CHAPTER FOUR

The Wounds of War: Unique Challenges for Wounded War Veterans and Their Families

"Have I not commanded you? Be strong and coura-
geous. Do not be terrified; do not be discouraged, for the
LORD your God will be with you wherever you go."
—Joshua 1:9 NIV

The Fear and Reality of Being Wounded

As families prepare to say goodbye to a soldier leaving for war, there is always an unspoken or rarely spoken subject that remains paramount in their thoughts: "What if my loved one does not return, or what if he comes home with war-related injuries?" Generations of soldiers and their families have clung together for one last hug prior to the soldier leaving with his or her unit for war. Hundreds of years ago they left by foot or on horseback with their weapon firmly attached to their body. Today most soldiers leave by bus or plane. Even though our current wars are fought with more sophistication and we no longer say goodbye to our soldier as he mounts a horse, the fear for our loved one's safety remains the same. We all want our loved one to return home safe and sound.

Of course, there are no guarantees that they will remain safe. As much as families cling to their fervent hope, soldiers do get hurt. Their daughter may lose a limb or her eyesight. Their son may come back minus his legs. Many families don't want to talk about this possibility because they feel it may jinx their loved one or cause an injury to happen.

My son Jeff left for Afghanistan when he had just turned 22. Originally I was supportive of his decision. His father had been in Vietnam and Jeff was proud of his service. He wanted to be just like his dad. When he was a senior in high school a Marine recruiter came to his school. Jeff was immediately hooked. He came home excited and bubbling over with enthusiasm about becoming a Marine. We helped him fill out the stack of papers and gave him our blessing for the journey that lay ahead. But when he was called up for deployment, I started having doubts. Afghanistan was so far away, and there was a chance he could be hurt or killed. I tried talking to my husband, but he did not want to discuss it. I tried talking to my friends about the "what if's" and they too changed the subject. Finally I decided that I should stop worrying.

Jeff left on a balmy spring day. He looked so handsome in his uniform that I was choked up with tears of happiness. But behind the first layer of tears were tears of fear. Even though I tried, I could not stop thinking about what I would do if he were hurt or killed. I hated when the phone rang because maybe it was a call saying he had been hurt. When the doorbell rang, I practically jumped under the bed so I would not have to see two uniformed officers waiting to tell me Jeff had been killed. I started playing games with myself. I became very superstitious. If I saw a red car on the way to work, he would be O.K. If I had five new emails that day, Jeff would be fine. I became more fearful. And no one would talk to me about it.

Finally a call did come. Jeff had been involved in a roadside bomb explosion. He was being transferred to

Germany. I seemed to quit breathing, and the world I knew seemed to stop. But then I sprang into action. We had to get expedited passports to go overseas, make flight arrangements, take leaves from our jobs, and find a place for the dogs. Finally we made it to Jeff's bedside. It was so wonderful to touch his hair and kiss his face. His legs and arms were the most damaged. He would need many surgeries and months and months of physical therapy. There was no guarantee that he would walk again or even that he would be able to keep his legs. But he was alive! We were in Germany with Jeff for almost ten days. Eventually he was transferred to a military hospital in the States. We faithfully followed him there.

I would like to say it is all better now, but I can't. There are still many uphill battles to face. When I think back on our experience, I wish I had been allowed to talk about my real fears of injury or death for Jeff. Because then I may have been able to brace myself for it or at least have acknowledged my fears. It seems that family and friends are reluctant to talk about the possibility that their loved one may be hurt or killed because if they talk about it they may cause it to happen. So they deny its existence. But sometimes it happens anyway.

Being injured in war is a traumatic and life-changing experience, not just for the soldier, but for his or her entire family. The person who left is not the person who came home.

What Types of Wounds Do Soldiers Face?

Wounds kill soldiers. In World War II more than 23 percent of U.S. troops who were wounded eventually died of those wounds. In Vietnam approximately 17 percent of wounded troops died. Today in Iraq that percentage has dropped to 9 percent of wounded troops dying ("The Wounded Come Home," Mark Thompson, *Time Magazine*, 2003). Fewer people dying from wounds means more people are living with them. And troops are living with a multitude of wounds that can cause enormous changes in their lives.

Major advances have helped save the lives of soldiers. There is better overall protection, mobile surgical care units, and quicker evacuation to hospitals. Soldiers are wearing Kevlar helmets and Kevlar vests. These helmets and vests are able to protect both the head and heart. They cannot protect the limbs of the soldiers, which is why many of the current injuries involve arms and legs.

More than 45 percent of the injuries received in Iraq involve the legs. Another 19 percent involve the arms ("The Wounded Come Home," Mark Thompson, *Time Magazine*, 2003). Many times, injuries affect both the arms and legs. Soldiers often undergo numerous surgeries, prosthetics, and months of physical therapy. Soldiers have to reconcile who they were with who they have become, and for some soldiers that can be a long journey.

Mobile surgical units are saving lives on a daily basis. Most deaths from injuries occur within the first hour after the injury, often because of loss of blood. Mobile surgical units consist of orthopedic surgeons, emergency physicians, anesthetists, and nurses. As the name suggests, they are a mobile team equipped to provide on-site care. Taking medical assistance to the soldier saves precious time, time that is often the difference between life and death.

Once an injured soldier is stabilized, she is usually evacuated to Landstuhl Regional Medical Center in Germany. This medical center, the only American hospital in Europe, further stabilizes the patient. The patient usually stays anywhere from three days to three weeks. At the end of this stay, the injured are either returned to continue their deployment or transferred to the United States for further medical treatment.

If they are moved to the United States, they will often go to Walter Reed Army Hospital in Washington, D.C. Other sites for continued treatment include Brooke Army Medical

Center in Texas or Bethesda Naval Hospital located in Maryland. Once she arrives in the United States, the soldier has a case manager assigned to her. The case manager's role is to coordinate medical treatment for the soldier and to help her plan for the future. The future may include being returned to active duty, or it may mean being honorably discharged from the military with disability pay.

The average length of stay at Walter Reed is six months. For many soldiers, half of that time is devoted to the healing process, while the other half of their stay focuses on learning to live with their injuries. For a soldier who has lost a limb, this means trying to imagine life with a prosthesis and not his or her "real limb." Vast improvements have been made in prosthetic devices, including prosthetic legs and arms that know how to bend because of sophisticated built-in microprocessors. Advancements in technology have allowed injured soldiers to rebuild their lives in a more normal way. They still have artificial limbs, but the line between artificial and real is growing thinner each day.

"At first I was very angry and depressed," states Jill, a petite 25-year-old blonde woman who lost an arm and part of a leg due to a roadside bomb in Iraq. As a truck driver she faced dangers on a daily basis, and she knew the risk of hitting an IED (improvised explosive device) was very real. "We all were aware of the risk, but what were we supposed to do? It was our job and our mission." The day of the actual bomb explosion is a blur in Jill's mind. She faintly recalls blue skies, dust, loud noises, pain, and chaos. When she finally realized what had happened, she was already in Germany. "I awoke in a daze, not really sure where I was or what happened to me. As my brain took in the bed, the sheets, the drawn shades, and many tubes hooked up to me, I realized I was in a hospital, but I was not sure why. And then my parents entered the room. One look at their stricken and shocked faces made me realize something awful had happened to me. It was then I noticed or rather sensed a change in my body. I peeked under the sheets. One of my arms was missing and most of my left leg was gone. I was missing two limbs! I broke down in sobs. How was I ever going to live again?"

But live again these soldiers do. Most soldiers "carry on" in exemplary, soldiering fashion. They usually don't wallow in self-pity for long. Dr. Harold Wain, a Walter Reed psychiatrist, in a November 3, 2003, *Time* article, "The Wounded Come Home," states, "They don't see it as a problem; they see it as a challenge. These soldiers are very proud of what they've done, and they don't want people to feel sorry for them. They want people to support them."

Wounded soldiers have access to state-of-the-art prosthesis and rehabilitation facilities. Once they are stabilized and treated at a military hospital, they are released to their home state. Remaining care is often picked up in their state through the local Veteran's Administration Hospital or through a local hospital. How long they receive treatment or how well they recover often depends on the injuries and the motivation of the soldier.

Physical injuries are real to soldiers and their families. Missing a leg or arm is an obvious injury. Burn scars and broken jaws are noticeable and real. But what about the emotional scars? What about the hidden scars of TBI (Traumatic Brain Injury) or PTSD (Post Traumatic Stress Disorder)? Soldiers who bear these injuries may look normal, but their behavior would often suggest otherwise. These are soldiers who start sweating profusely in large crowds as they scan the room to find a safe exit. These are soldiers who dive under the living room table when they hear a car backfire or who react erratically when someone passes near them on a busy interstate. These so-called "invisible injuries" have increased substantially during the Iraq war. Because others cannot see them, these afflictions are especially difficult for soldiers to deal with. And because they are not seen, they are often not understood by others.

Understanding Invisible Injuries

Invisible injuries usually involve the brain and include a variety of symptoms and diagnoses including TBI (Traumatic Brain Injury). Despite Kevlar helmets, soldiers are at an increased risk for TBIs. These injuries are caused from the shock waves that accompany explosions. For example, soldiers traveling in vehicle convoys are at risk from roadside bombs. When a bomb detonates, the explosion can cause traumatic brain injuries to persons in the vicinity of the blast.

Because traumatic brain injuries are not apparent from the outside, doctors must rely on brain scans and an assessment of the soldier's behaviors. Many families note that their soldier is displaying "different behaviors that are out of character" for their loved one. These behaviors include constant headaches, sleep disturbances, sensitivity to light, difficulty paying attention, memory loss, mood swings, and depression. Because these symptoms also mimic post traumatic stress disorder, it is sometimes hard to distinguish between the two conditions, which can and do frequently overlap.

Many of the wounded soldiers who go through Landstuhl Medical Center in Germany have some form of brain injury in addition to their various physical injuries. Despite the obvious challenges soldiers face with physical injuries, many struggle as much or more with their invisible injuries. Soldiers with traumatic brain injuries sometimes feel they are "going crazy" and are unsure why they are struggling so much in their lives. Their families also observe changes.

> Tom came home from Iraq looking refreshed and renewed. We were amazed. We thought he would look different somehow. We expected him to look older or tougher or somehow damaged. We knew he had been involved with a roadside bomb, but the truck he was

riding in had been at least seven trucks behind the one that had been hit. Just as a precaution he was checked out by a military doctor in Iraq but was deemed "fit." He went back to his work with seemingly no problems. One month later his tour was done and he came home. At first we did not notice anything different. He was a bit impatient and somewhat forgetful, but we chalked it up to learning how to readjust to his job as a loan officer. But little by little we noticed bigger things. He was not sleeping very well. He complained often of headaches, and no amount of pain medications made them go away. Bright lights and sunlight seemed to make him edgy, and he was always seeking out shaded areas and darkened rooms. Worst of all his personality seemed to change. He was moody and angry. Things he used to love doing no longer brought him pleasure. He would not fish with his friends nor bowl with his father. He was always restless and anxious. Finally we convinced him to go to the VA for a physical. After many tests he was diagnosed with Traumatic Brain Injury. In a way we were relieved. Now we had a name for what we were experiencing, and we could finally understand how to help him.

Treatment for traumatic brain injury often revolves around rehabilitation. Depending on the symptoms, the soldier can receive physical, occupational, or speech therapy. He or she also can be helped with medications and counseling.

Another invisible wound is PTSD (Post Traumatic Stress Disorder). This disorder is defined as "a psychological response to the experience of intense traumatic events, particularly those that threaten life" (*PTSD and the Family*, Veterans Affairs Canada, 2006). According to this booklet, there are three groups of problems that are found with PTSD: intrusive, avoidance, and arousal symptoms. Someone who has PTSD can relive the traumatic experience again and again. He or she lives with continual anxiety, knowing that certain smells, foods, sights, or sounds may trigger traumatic memories.

> We were relieved when Jose finally got home. As a
> Marine Reservist he had been in some pretty fierce fight-
> ing, and his dad and I worried that he might have some
> trouble forgetting both what he saw and did. He was dis-
> tant at first, but slowly he seemed to get back into a rou-
> tine. He enrolled in school and started to date.
> Everything seemed pretty normal. And then one day we
> were all sitting in the backyard. The kids next door set off
> a firecracker. In mid-sentence Jose jumped up and ran
> behind the wood pile. He was shaking all over, and sweat
> was pouring off his face.

People who suffer from traumatic events usually don't
want to talk about what happened. They usually avoid
thinking about the event and try to keep it buried. They
have found that if they talk about the event, they are, in a
sense, forced to relive it, and reliving it is too painful. So
they numb their emotions and withdraw. They don't show
sadness or grief, but they also don't show happiness and
excitement.

Being constantly on guard is another common symptom.
People with PTSD may become jumpy and on edge. Danger
seems to lurk everywhere and they feel that they have to
"be ready" at any time. This arousal state is with them both
day and night, which means they often have trouble con-
centrating and sleeping.

Getting On with Life

Wounds alter the soldiers and their families. Both are different from who they were. Soldiers may be missing legs
and be blind in one eye. They may have permanent memory loss that affects their day-to-day living. With such rad-
ical changes, it is not surprising that one of the biggest
challenges the wounded soldier and his or her family face
is learning to get on with a changed life.

It is important to remember that the injured soldier is part of a family. His or her recovery will take place within the context of that family. The soldier is the one who has to undergo the surgeries and physical therapy, but the entire family is affected. They must be valued for their roles and respected for their ideas. Once the soldier has been stabilized and has completed his rehabilitation, he is released to the care of the family and their hospital or Veterans Administration system.

What happens to the soldier upon release? What comes next for the soldier who is not only released from the military hospital but also released from the service with disability pay? What becomes of the soldier who is no longer fit for duty? A report released by the Wounded Warrior program in 2008 states that most injured soldiers go through various stages of emotional recovery. They often start with a period of denial, followed by anger. As the anger wanes, soldiers may enter a stage in which they try to bargain to regain what they have lost. Depression, the fourth stage, often follows when the soldier learns the injuries are real and that she will need to make permanent changes because of them.

Acceptance is the next stage. During this stage soldiers learn to accept who they have become and start to move on with their lives. The normalizing stage is when soldiers start to develop life routines based on their current situations. Thriving is the final stage, in which the soldier can become a role model to others because of how he or she has overcome the challenges.

People go through these stages according to their own timeline. Even though recovery is depicted as a linear process, in reality it is more circular. Soldiers go back and forth between stages and, in some instances, skip stages altogether.

Grief and loss dictate the soldier's recovery process and affect the family as well. The soldier now has to define himself as a "different person." Initially, most wounded soldiers identify themselves as who they were as opposed to who they have become through injuries.

"I came home from Iraq as a wounded soldier," states Austin, a 26-year-old father of three. "I left as a proud soldier who led convoys through some of the roughest stretches of road in Iraq. I had two months left of my tour when our Humvee blew up. I lost both arms and part of a leg. Eight whole months have passed and yet when someone asks me, 'What do you do?' I initially answer, 'I am a soldier in the infantry division.' Sometimes they stare at me with a confused look on their face. Usually I correct myself and say, 'Oh, I *was* a soldier.' But it is hard. All I ever wanted to be was a soldier."

As the soldier comes to grips with his or her losses, the family too is trying to make sense of the new person in their lives and how the injuries affect him or her. Injuries can cause a lot of disruptions in the family. There are structural changes when a house has to be altered to allow a person with handicaps to maneuver through the house. There can be financial strains as the family faces loss of income due to the injury. It may be necessary for the family to move so they can be closer to hospitals or rehabilitation centers. There may be changes in roles.

Children also struggle with the changes. They have to learn to reconcile that their dad will never be able to run a race with them again. They have to make a new image of their mom because their "new" mom is unable to remember basic information and always has to write things down. Children will vary in their degree of understanding. Their age and developmental stages will have great bearing on how well they can accept their injured parent and how they too can get on with their lives.

Military Support for Injured Soldiers

AW2 (Army Wounded Warrior Program) is the official Army program that serves severely wounded, injured, and ill soldiers and their families as long as it takes. Each soldier in this program is assigned an AW2 Advocate and also to a

Warrior Transition Unit (WTU) to focus on healing. The advocate provides personalized, local support with no time limitations, regardless of location or military status. He or she also assists wounded soldiers and their families with benefit information, career guidance, educational opportunities, and financial audits.

In addition to the AW2 program, there are a multitude of programs that can help soldiers and their families adjust to their current situation. They are as follows:

National Center for PTSD: www.ncptsd.va.gov
Vet Center: www.vetcenter.va.gov
Wounded Warrior Program: www.aw2.army.mil
Military One Source: www.militaryonesource.com
Veterans Benefits Administration: www.vab.va.gov
Defense and Veterans Brain Injury Center: www.dvbic.org

Concluding Thoughts

Becoming wounded in war shatters many assumptions about life and plans for the future. Soldiers who thought they were invincible or at least lucky enough to avoid injury have had their illusions destroyed. Family members who thought they would be greeting an airplane or bus with bands playing as their loved one came home find a different reality facing them, that of trying to help their loved one rehabilitate and recover from the wounds of war. It often calls for serious remodeling of one's life to accommodate new limitations after being wounded.

Remodeling a life is a lot like remodeling a home that has been hit by a storm or ravaged by fire. The task is to make it livable again. Often the owners are overwhelmed by the calamity that befell them and need time to process the grief and loss of that event. First, they take a walk through the house to see what can be done to fix the situation. Some broken parts of the house may have to be torn down and removed before they can build something new. Some things like old appliances that don't work anymore can be tossed out, along with debris from the fire or storm. Then, we want to determine what can be salvaged from the damage or transformed into a good thing (like knocking out a wall to make a more spacious kitchen). Last, we decide what new furnishings we want to bring in to enhance the home and make it attractive and functional.

When recovering from the wounds of war, soldiers and their families have to assess what goes or stays in their lives, what works and does not work in the aftermath of being wounded. They have to decide what can be transformed, remodeled, or changed to accommodate living a good life within limitations and with the resources available. And then they begin to dream again of a new life that brings joy and purpose.

Tips for Ministry

- Each family and soldier adjusts in their own way. Patience, kindness, and compassion go a long way during their struggles. Sometimes it is not what is said but rather what is done that helps the most. Think of how to help the family. Are there little children at home? Offer some regular babysitting volunteers to help watch the children while the parents take care of business, go to therapy, or just get away together.
- Provide opportunities for the families to talk with a pastor, with other vets, and in church. They have a powerful story to tell.
- Wounded soldiers and their families usually don't want sympathy, but they do want our respect and support. Be aware of how the church can accommodate an injured person. If the soldier is in a wheelchair, will he or she be able to get around the church or are there structural barriers? If there are barriers, can they be removed?

CHAPTER FIVE

Comforting Those Who Mourn: Ministering to Families of Military Casualties

Religion that God our Father accepts as pure and fault-less is this: to look after orphans and widows in their distress and to keep oneself from being polluted by the world. —James 1:27 NIV

A United States Marine had lost his life in the service of his country. The Marine Casualty Officer and I, a Navy chaplain, attired in dress uniforms, pulled into the drive-way of the family's home at 9:00 A.M. Both of us, in spite of years of military experience, were nervous about what was going to happen in the next few moments. The time had come to deliver devastating news that would change the lives of a military family forever.

We rang the doorbell and waited. The door opened and behind the screen door was the wife of the Marine, stand-ing holding a cup of coffee. She took one look at us and before we could say a word she knew why we had come. She cried, "No," and then threw a cupful of hot coffee through the screen door, spraying hot coffee over us. She slammed the door in our face, trying to shut the bad news out. We rang the doorbell again, and after several minutes, a neighbor, who had stopped by for a cup of coffee that morning, opened the door and invited us in. We relayed to the woman the limited information we had about the death of her husband and then left with heavy hearts. In the days and weeks that followed, I would recall the image of that young widow with her two toddlers snuggling up to her on the couch as she quietly sobbed. It was the toughest duty I had ever done.

Everyone who puts on a uniform knows there is a chance that he or she could be killed in combat, in training, or in other accidents while serving in the military. All military personnel have to fill out paperwork noting next of kin to notify in case of death in the line of duty. They all have to have updated wills drawn up before deploying and are reminded to update beneficiaries on life insurance policies. If they own homes, property, or have any dependent children, they may draw up appropriate powers of attorney. For most, the idea is remote that they will be killed or badly injured, but it is there in the back of their mind.

The Human Cost of War

Military service is dangerous. Service personnel may be injured or killed in combat or in line-of-duty accidents. From World War I to the present, 641,254 service personnel have died in uniform and 1,216,218 have been wounded in action. The ratio of killed to wounded has, in recent years, decreased significantly. In World War II, for every soldier killed, 1.5 soldiers (1:1.5 ratio) were wounded. Today, largely due to improved body armor and medical interventions, soldiers who would have died from wounds in the past now live. In the current armed conflicts, the killed to wounded ratio is 1:7, indicating higher survival in combat (DOD Personnel & Procurement Statistics, April 2009):

> This means that many veterans return to our communities dealing with the profound loss of physical and men-

tal abilities due to war. Many families of soldiers killed in our wars are grieving this loss and trying to adjust to life without their loved one. It is important to understand the magnitude of the losses in war and the grief many family members suffered and are currently suffering as a result of a service-connected death or disability.

The Military Care of Casualties

In modern warfare, when a soldier is wounded or injured, the U.S. military makes great efforts and spares no expense to save the life of that soldier. From the point of injury, with the immediate emergency services of medical corps personnel, through field hospitals where doctors and nurses stabilize a soldier, to medical air evacuation to major military hospitals where the best trauma, surgical, and long-term rehabilitation services are rendered, every effort is made to save a soldier's life.

Today, with the chances of a soldier surviving wounds in battle being so much greater than being killed, grief and loss more often involve the challenges of coping with disabling wounds than with death. As soldiers rehabilitate from devastating amputations or brain injuries, they and their families have to change their assumptions about life; they have to cope as individuals and as families with challenging disabilities.

The impact of a serious combat-related disability on the family of a service person can lead to feelings of deep loss of the future that was planned (a death of dreams). There is a continuing grief as family members begin to realize what life will be like for themselves as well as for their soldier. This disenfranchised grief, which is often not socially recognized or publicly mourned, becomes part of a lifetime of care-giving for families of wounded soldiers.

In war, soldiers die! Death in combat or by military accident is not "normal" death; it is the untimely death of a young person. It is not the same kind of grief associated with the death of someone in their nineties, surrounded by family and friends as they slip away. In an era of modern artillery, mortars, and mines, death usually is sudden, violent, and often dismembering. Military personnel who fly or are transported in helicopters and fixed-wing aircraft are subject to ground fire and mechanical problems that may cause them to crash and burn, making recovery of intact bodies difficult. Aviators shot down over enemy territory or those who crash at sea may be listed forever as missing in action (MIA).

When a solder, sailor, airman, marine, or coast guard personnel is killed in the line of duty, the military services go to great lengths to assist family members: they make timely notifications of family members; assist them with funeral preparations, including military honors; and assign a casualty affairs officer to them to make sure the family receives all the benefits and assistance due to them in the aftermath of a service-connected death.

Once a death is confirmed in a combat theater, every effort is made to notify the next of kin quickly. A notification officer and chaplain make a personal call on primary next of kin, informing them of the death and beginning to offer assistance with funeral and decedent affairs issues. The military prepares the body, which is then placed in full dress uniform in a casket. The body is flown to the city or town the family designates for the funeral and the burial. They offer, if the family desires, full military honors at the gravesite (military pallbearers, firing squad, and bugler) and a military chaplain if requested. The casualty affairs officer (CAO) stays in touch with the family as long as they need his or her assistance in applying for military benefits and other assistance. These CAOs, assigned this very difficult duty, carry it out with the care, compassion, and outstanding professionalism that helps a fallen soldier's family at one of the most difficult times of their life.

Soldiers and Their Families Are Acquainted with Grief

Military families of casualties are already acquainted with grief long before notification of a combat injury or death. Everyone has a grief history prior to entering the military community: prior deaths of family members and losses among extended family related to divorce, job loss, and disability. Military families have gone through the grief of saying goodbye as troops deploy; they have lived with the anxiety and fear of something horrible happening. How family members handled past grief and loss experiences in life and the tools they bring to a new grief experience from those times will greatly influence how they will respond to a casualty notification.

A unique feature of combat death is its suddenness and violence, complicating the grieving process, making it more intense. Sudden deaths create a "sense of unreality, guilt, need to blame, helplessness, unfinished business with survivor, and an increased need to understand" (Worden, 1991, pp. 98-100). No one likes surprises, and news of a combat death, even though one has anticipated that it could happen, comes as a shock that is hard to accept and adjust to quickly.

Usually, persons whose loved one suffered a combat death experience complicated bereavement. Here the grief is more intense and lasts much longer than "normal" grief. Some of the characteristics of complicated grief reactions are valuable to know to assist grieving military family members in getting help for themselves. Dr. William Worden, in his book *Grief Counseling and Grief Therapy*, explains how grief goes wrong in four negative ways: "*Chronic, delayed, exaggerated, and masked grief reactions*" (Worden, 1991, pp. 71-74).

1. Chronic grief reactions: Grief that never ends. The person is feeling unfinished after years of grieving and is very aware that this is going on.

2. Delayed grief reactions: Postponed grief. Here personal grief is suppressed at the time of a loss to attend to practical survival issues or assist others in coping, to the neglect of self. At a later date, grief comes back, often triggered by another loss (divorce, job loss, absence of deceased parent at wedding), and the reaction is more intense than at the time of the triggering event that caused the reaction.
3. Exaggerated grief reactions: A person feels overwhelmed in grief and resorts to pathological behavior (i.e., clinical unipolar or bipolar depression, anxiety/panic attacks, and serious alcohol and substance abuse).
4. Masked grief reactions: Persons may not allow themselves to experience grief directly, but instead develop medical problems, psychosomatic complaints, or psychiatric symptoms. They have no clue as to the linkage of the problem to the grief event.

In my experience as a grief counselor and chaplain working with grieving military family members, all of the above-mentioned grief reactions are common, with chronic grief reactions most common after a traumatic death. For many family members, it takes a very long time for intense mourning to subside. Chronic heaviness in the chest and frequent sudden temporary upsurges in grief (STUG) reactions persisting for several years are commonly reported. Some spouses with children and a lot of responsibility for others stoically lay aside their normal grief reactions to care for others and fall victim to delayed grief reaction.

A key issue in helping military families in bereavement is to assess the support systems they have available to them at this difficult time. Families that have a strong network of extended family, friends, and faith community appear to do much better at coping and being resilient after a combat death. Lack of social support after a loss is an indicator of high risk for pathological mourning for survivors.

The Tasks of Mourning

What can we do to assist a person mourning the loss of a soldier? How do we help veterans' families, maybe years after a war, to mourn in a healthy way?

There are four tasks of mourning generally agreed upon that grieving military families need to accomplish to complete the process of mourning: "They need to accept the reality of the loss, work through the pain of grief, adjust to an environment in which the deceased is missing, and emotionally relocate the deceased and move on with life" (Worden, 1991, pp. 10-16).

Acceptance of a loss is often one of the most difficult parts of dealing with the deaths of service personnel. They were young and vibrant, with so much of their lives before them. This grief involves loss of dreams for an expected future by family members. The soldiers were physically absent from their families, so their deaths feel unreal. Many families have a hard time believing the death has happened. This is particularly exacerbated if the service person is missing in action (MIA) but presumed dead. Without a body for reviewing, it is easier to slip into denial that the event really happened; family members believe there has been a terrible mix-up somehow. If there has been an ambivalent relationship between the deceased and a family member, the survivor may discount the loss.

Working through the pain of grief involves feeling the pain of loss. There is a tendency to try not to feel bad, to either idealize the deceased beyond recognition or to think only about pleasant aspects of life and never admit the emotional train wreck being experienced. Some people avoid the negative feelings of mourning by eliminating triggers that prompt memories of the deceased, donating possessions, and erasing reminders of him or her.

Adjusting to a life with the soldier forever missing is challenging. It means recognizing finally that the soldier is not coming back. It can also mean managing finances on a diminished income, raising children as a single parent, and missing all the other roles the soldier played in the life of the family.

For a spouse it means learning new skills and making a new future. It means emotionally dealing with the empty bed and the quiet house. If the family resided in military quarters, there are practical issues of moving. It means getting new ID cards for the surviving spouse and children and starting over in so many ways. There is often an initial period of support offered by the military right after a death, but then there is a growing sense of not belonging to the military community anymore. The family is faced with starting over in a civilian world again, perhaps getting more education to get a job that will support the family on a single income. It means coping with a sense of loss of direction in life and changing some assumptions about how the world works. It means making decisions alone at a time when a person feels most vulnerable and incapable. For some, it means wrestling with hard questions about God and coming to peace spiritually.

Emotionally relocating the deceased and moving on with life is the final stage leading to completed mourning. This means re-engaging with life and with people and redirecting emotional energy that has focused only on the deceased. Of course, family members continue to think about the loved one who died in the line of duty, but they find a quiet place to put them in their hearts without letting that loss dominate their thinking every moment of the day. It means reinvesting in life and doing so as a way of honoring the loved one lost. For some spouses, it means loving again, being open to finding another life partner with whom to continue life's journey. Individuals have not completed this step if they refuse to move on after a period of time and instead choose to let all of life stop at the death of the soldier they loved.

When is grief done? That all depends on the individual's personality, the depth of the relationship with the deceased, and the coping skills and support systems they possess. This process can last from at least two years to as much as five years, certainly not the time usually allocated for bereavement. Completed grief is usually seen when a person is able to think of the deceased without pain. That means it is a journey where time has to be a friend and where a person, at his or her own pace, and especially with the help of a caring faith community, finds a new place to belong and become.

Parents and Siblings of Veterans

Often, there is a lot of attention focused on spouses and children of service personnel lost in action, with little attention paid to parents and siblings. For a parent, the loss of a son or daughter is the loss of a future. A whole set of hopes and dreams that is part of the assumptive world of a parent simply jolts to a halt. A future with grandchildren is gone (for the parent of a young soldier with no children) or the role of being a grandparent greatly diminished; the spouse of the son or daughter may move away with the children and eventually remarry. Their pride in the success of their soldier is forever fixed in time, with no further entries to be made—no new celebrations, no new photos for the family album. Concerns of growing old and not having that son or daughter for support may be troubling. Some of the joy of life is gone, and often they struggle with the thought that the best of times has passed. Unless parents are helped through the tasks of mourning, life will be diminished for them in ways they never imagined when they waved good-bye to their son or daughter. Their physical and mental health may suffer if the sadness continues and they can't find a reason to get well. It is of great importance for the community of faith to uphold these parents in prayer and offer them ways to reinvest in life and find some meaning and purpose after their loss.

Siblings who played together as children and have shared memories with the lost brother or sister need time to mourn as well. Losing a brother or sister underlines the fragility of life for young adults; this can sometimes lead to constructive or destructive choices for siblings. They have lost a contemporary, a friend and confidant, who would have accompanied them through all the stages of life and supported them in times of trouble and celebrated with them in times of joy. They too have lost part of the future they expected to have.

Children and Grief

A special word needs to be said about the children of those service personnel who die in the line of duty. One of the hardest things for chaplains who officiate at military funerals is to look at the young children who cling to mom or dad as the firing squad fires their volleys and taps is played over the grave of their dead parent. They are wondering what will happen to them now.

Children also need to accept the reality of the loss. The approach to telling a child a parent has died depends on the child's age and the ability to understand. It is normal for them to experience a range of emotions: anger, sadness, guilt, and anxiety. If there have been conflicts in the relationship between the children and the deceased parent, young children may feel the death is their fault, or children who were very close to the parent may question why they were abandoned. Children need time to adjust to an environment where the deceased is missing, adapting best if the remaining parent is grieving appropriately. Some children in military families have grown used to an absent parent; it may take many months before those children realize "Mom (or Dad) is never coming home." Sometimes there is a delayed grief reaction, and, at significant events, like graduations or weddings, the "child" is suddenly filled with grief for the parent who has been gone for years. Children also need to relocate the dead person within their life and find appropriate ways to memorialize him or her.

Research indicates that boys are more affected by the loss of a parent than the loss of a sibling. "Preteen boys who lost a parent were more withdrawn, more anxious and depressed, and tended to show more somatic symptoms than those who lost a sibling. Father loss in boys was an important contributor to risk during the first year of bereavement. In contrast, girls were more affected (in the same way) by the loss of a sibling" (Worden, 1991, p. 122). How the surviving parent coped with the loss has a significant role in how children fare in grief: if the parent does well, the children do well, and if the parent does not, neither do the children. So, for those involved in congregational care, it is important to invest resources in guarding the functioning and well-being of the surviving parent, and the children will usually respond positively.

Resources

Because death in combat or by military accident in the line of duty presents very unique challenges to churches, pastors, and congregational care teams that minister to military families, it is important to mention some key resources and support connections that can help.

- The best book for military widows and those who minister to them: *Military Widow—A Survival Guide*, by Joanne M. Steen & M. Regina Asaro (Annapolis, Md.: Naval Institute Press, 2006).
- Support and assistance for bereaved military families: Gold Star Mothers, www.goldstarmoms.com, (202) 265-0991, and Gold Star Wives, http://www.goldstarwives.org, and Tragedy

Assistance Program for Survivors (TAPS), http://www.taps.org.

- Bereavement counseling for military families of veterans KIA: Veterans Readjustment Counseling Services (202) 273-9116 and Military OneSource (800) 342-9647.
- Funeral Planning: The Department of Defense website on "Military Funeral Honors" has information for families and clergy to receive help with arranging a veteran's funeral: http://www.mili taryfuneralhonors.osd.mil.

Concluding Thoughts

The spiritual challenges facing military families after the death of a loved one are daunting. Like all of us, at moments of grief they ask: "Why God?" "Why me?" "Why do bad things happen to good people?" "How can this be God's will?"

Military families who grieve struggle with the same questions we all wrestle with in times of tragedy. They need to be included in the outreach and concern of the care ministries of the church, not unlike the widow who lost her husband to cancer or a young mother who through divorce is suddenly single and overwhelmed. As we have been comforted and supported by friends and the community of faith, we extend that same comfort to military families in our communities who have lost a son or daughter, a husband or wife, or mom or dad in war.

Paul the apostle reminds us that the soul wound of grief can ultimately only be healed by God's hand through God's people: "Praise be to the God and Father of our Lord Jesus Christ, the Father of compassion and the God of all comfort, who comforts us in all our troubles, so that we can comfort those in any trouble with the comfort we ourselves have received from God" (2 Cor. 1:3-4 NIV).

Tips for Ministry

- Identify veterans' families in your church and community who are living with service-connected injuries or death and seek to reach out to them with your care ministries.
- Provide a format (maybe Memorial Day or Veterans Day) to have veterans and families tell their stories and help them memorialize their losses.
- Learn about appropriate resources to share with parents, siblings, and spouses that have lost a loved one in uniform and share them with those who mourn.
- Contact your National Guard State Chaplain for information on officiating protocols if required to perform a military funeral for active service personnel or a veteran.
- Support the outreach services of Gold Star Mothers and Gold Star Wives and the work of TAPS (Tragedy Assistance Program for Survivors) in caring for bereaved family members of service personnel killed in our wars.

CHAPTER SIX

Onward Christian Soldiers: Moral and Spiritual Issues Facing Soldiers and Their Families

And what does the LORD require of you? To act justly and to love mercy and to walk humbly with your God.
—Micah 6:8 NIV

War is hard on the human spirit. Our soldiers go into the service because they want to preserve and protect the country that they love. They have to be intensively trained to be able to take someone's life. Either the anticipation of that life-taking act or participation in killing can harm a person's spiritual health. Some veterans, in anguish over what they have done in war, need to experience forgiveness and grace. Pastors, chaplains, and church leaders can be a great help to veterans in dealing with these serious ethical issues.

A Moral Dilemma

A weapons officer on a nuclear ballistic submarine faced an ethical dilemma. He had repeatedly deployed on 90-day nuclear deterrence patrols under the Pacific Ocean. He had never been shot at or, in turn, shot at anyone in anger. He had not experienced the tensions of a combat soldier shooting it out with insurgents in a firefight in Iraq or

Afghanistan. He was responsible, however, if the president directed and his commanding officer ordered him to launch Trident missiles, with multiple individually targeted 100-kiloton nuclear warheads on each missile, that would devastate a whole country and kill millions of people.

The naval officer reported that every patrol lately had become filled with moral tension for him, as he repeatedly practiced simulated launches preparing for doing the "real thing," bringing nuclear winter upon the world. And even though he had a job far from the front lines, he felt a growing moral dilemma over his role and mission. The ethical conflict finally drove him to resign from the service to find peace in his heart.

Everyone who deals with nuclear weapons in the Air Force Air Combat Command (ACC), the Air Force Space Command (AFSPC), or the Navy nuclear ballistic missile submarine deterrence force regularly practices and prepares for nuclear war. Even though they may be far from contemporary war front lines, the stresses and moral dilemmas weigh upon the spirit.

To best understand the ethical tensions Christians face being involved in military service and warfare, it is important to briefly review the teachings of the Christian church in this area. How do those Christian teachings on war and peace conflict with the kinds of situations service members encounter?

Christian Teaching on War and Peace

If one is going to enter into a caring relationship with a soldier or family member who is having ethical problems about fighting in a war, it is appropriate to have a basic understanding of how the Christian church has viewed this issue. There are many books on the subject from differing perspectives that inquiring Christians can read to expand their knowledge of the issues to prepare for such an encounter. For our brief discussion, we will only outline two of the most prominent approaches in Christian ethics regarding participation in war: Christian nonviolence (pacifism) and just war theory.

Christian Nonviolence (Pacifist) Position

The Christian nonviolence position views any form of violence as incompatible with the Christian faith. This position argues that Jesus taught nonviolence and that the early church forbade violence as an option, even in self-defense. They argue that there is no evidence of "Christian soldiers" in the first 150 years of the church and serving in the army did not become an acceptable vocation until after A.D. 312, when Emperor Constantine became a Christian and the merging of church and state became an issue.

Pacifists would encourage Christians to embrace the stance of the early church, which avoided entanglements with politics. They don't believe that supporting nationalistic efforts justifies the violence that comes with war and military service. Leo Tolstoy and Martin Luther King, Jr. are modern examples of those who have held positions of Christian nonviolence, along with many members of peace churches (Mennonites and Quakers) and those from the Jehovah's Witnesses and Seventh Day Adventists.

Just War Theory

The other Christian position on participation in war is the just war theory, which allows participation of Christians in warfare under certain limiting conditions. These limiting conditions involve asking hard questions about each engagement and not merely giving blanket approval to war. A key question that is to be asked in all warfare situations is: Do the reasons for conflict seem justified in terms of the outcomes pursued, and are the means to achieve those ends congruent with exercising restraint in regard to noncombatant civilian populations?

Richard Falk, in his article "Defining a Just War" (*The Nation*, October 11, 2001), summarizes the most important ideas of this theory, drawn from just war traditions in theology, international law, and ideas of restraint in the world's religions. Its most important ideas are:

- The principle of discrimination: force must be directed at a military target, with damage to civilians and civilian society being incidental;
- The principle of proportionality: force must not be greater than that needed to achieve an acceptable military result and must not be greater than the provoking cause;
- The principle of humanity: force must not be directed against enemy personnel if they are subject to capture, wounded, or under control (as with prisoners of war);
- The principle of necessity: force should be used only if nonviolent means to achieve military goals are unavailable.

Christians, both those who hold a pacifist position and those who hold a just war position, regard war as human failure and the product of sinful actions and attitudes. War causes great pain and sorrow for humanity. The nonviolent position contends that participation in war is always incompatible with being a Christian, while the just war advocates take the position that sometimes Christians have to go to war to stop greater evil, but do so with sorrow in their hearts.

Political and Military Attitudes
toward War

Political and military views of national leaders generally regard war as an evil means that may justify a good end.

Much of what drives a nation's policy is a pragmatism that serves state security and national self-interest. It is a world-view that is more interested in what is effective rather than what is right or wrong on a moral plane. This philosophy is skeptical of using moral concepts to apply to the conduct of nation-states. Subscription to rules of war emanates more from a perspective of self-interest than from any moral teaching (i.e., we treat prisoners of war well so our captured soldiers won't be tortured by the enemy).

When service members who grew up in Christian communities join a military service, they are joining a secular organization that may not subscribe to the same standards of conduct expected of Christians. The military has a strong emphasis on core values. The seven core values of the Army are loyalty, duty, respect, self-sacrifice, honor, integrity, and personal courage. Coupled with these core values are the Laws of War that soldiers are required to follow in conducting themselves honorably on a battlefield. Many of these laws parallel the requirements of the just war position. But there are many areas where soldiers are caught up in the heat of battle in a very pragmatic and at times utilitarian organization that does not always easily mesh with Christian values. It is here where Christian soldiers are tested in their faith.

Also, in the fog of war, the practical challenges of combat come at soldiers with blinding speed, and they are required to make instant decisions on ethical and moral issues. If you have not considered these issues and adopted and practiced them in life before, it is pretty hard to reflexively make good, principled decisions in the heat of the battle.

Sometimes the choices military leaders have to make involve trying to make the best of a range of evil things—decisions that they will have a lifetime to critique like a Monday morning quarterback. All of us who have worn the uniform since the Nuremberg War Crimes trials at the end of World War II know that we cannot simply say, "I was just following orders." We are held personally responsible for our conduct in war and will be judged before God and humankind accordingly.

Ethics and the Fog of War

There are some situations that are pretty clear for soldiers to understand regarding their conduct in war: you don't torture or shoot prisoners, you avoid killing or wounding civilian noncombatants, you don't leave your wounded or dead comrades behind, and you take care to look after the well-being of fellow soldiers. Some situations are pretty unambiguous, while others are less so.

Unambiguous Ethical Situations in War

All killing is not the same in warfare. Sometimes it is defensive and soldiers have no choice but to kill those who are trying to kill them. Soldiers don't waste a lot of time agonizing over such acts. Even in offensive warfare, where one is attacking troops that are supporting evil causes, this kind of life-taking brings little angst to the hearts of military personnel. Soldiers initially may be shocked to see the carnage of battle, with casualties littered across a battlefield after combat. Over time they can become acclimated to such sights if they understand the reasons for fighting those battles and are able to view their actions as justified by stopping a greater evil or by defending themselves.

In the post–World War II era, where military interventions were made for humanitarian or peacekeeping actions with no eye to personal or national gain (like stopping pirates from hijacking ships at sea off the Somalian coast or participating in peacekeeping operations with NATO missions in Kosovo), there is little ethical struggle.

Ambiguous Ethical Situations

One conflict for service members comes where the act of war does not seem proportional or where many innocent noncombatants are killed. Most of these feelings about war, especially killing innocent women, children, and elderly people, haunt veterans for decades after a war. Most soldiers have a sense of right and wrong but can't put their finger on just why they feel some killing is righteous and some is not justifiable. As veterans, we remember that there are Laws of Warfare in the Uniform Code of Military Justice that define how a soldier should behave in a conflict. We know that before any combat operation commanders outline certain rules of engagement that are to govern behavior in battle.

One problem is that the battlefield is a messy place, where things happen rapidly and call for quick reactions. The moral dilemmas that service personnel face become very challenging, as enemy forces blend in with civilian populations and use them as cover from which to fire on advancing soldiers. When assaulting a position, soldiers often "double tap" enemy soldiers to make sure they are down, shooting at them twice to ensure their own safety in approaching enemy soldiers. This means, however, that enemy soldiers are rarely taken alive as wounded casualties to become prisoners of war.

The Impact of Distance upon the Act of Killing in War

Most human beings are not born to kill. It takes a lot of training to get soldiers to be willing to kill and to do it repeatedly. LTC Dave Grossman, in his book *On Killing*, outlines the impact of distance in providing a way to cope morally with doing this humanly unnatural act: distancing from the act of killing "mechanically, socially, culturally, and morally" (Grossman, 1996, p. 160).

Mechanical Distance
Few aviators are traumatized by what they see in war, because they are so physically distant from the damage

they do to their targets. Aviators drop bombs or fire rockets on enemy targets and, on occasion, hit civilians, producing what the military euphemistically calls "collateral damage." The moral tension decreases as bombs and missiles land on buildings seen only through video cameras, allowing the viewer little grasp of the carnage wrought on human lives. Like scenes we saw of the first Gulf War, the video scene looks like a Nintendo game that kids play on a computer screen, with little emotion tied to the explosions of laser-guided bombs or cruise missiles. The greater physical distance from those they killed in war provided combatants with greater insulation from having to grapple with the consequences of their actions. It was easier to repeat those actions again and again with little remorse or reflection.

Social Distance

Infantry soldiers see war up close and personal, at the point of impact of shooting or an explosion, or in the very presence of enemy combatants and civilians. They can see the toll of warfare at the bloody end of the spear. One way of dealing with killing is to put social distance between oneself and those being fought. As long as war is impersonal and soldiers don't think much about the "enemy" and just follow orders, there is little moral struggle about taking life. It is just "us" against "them." But let acts of war become personal, thinking about "the other" as being like oneself, someone's son or daughter with spouse and children waiting for them, and it becomes challenging to kill these people.

A veteran of World War II in the Pacific, now in his mid-eighties, reflected remorsefully on actions that took place some sixty-five years ago when he came face-to-face with a Japanese soldier in the jungle:

> I had my .45 [caliber pistol] in my hand and the point of his bayonet was no farther than you are to me when I shot him. After everything was settled down, I helped

search his body for intelligence purposes and found a photograph. It was a picture of his wife and these two beautiful children. Ever since (as tears began to roll down his cheeks), I have been haunted by the thought of these two beautiful children growing up without their father, because I murdered their daddy. I'm not a young man anymore, and soon I'll have to answer to my Maker for what I have done. (Grossman, 1996, p. 157)

Many aging veterans, with time on their hands to reflect on wartime memories, are struggling to understand some of the things they did in war, to make amends, or find peace with those experiences before they die.

Cultural Distance

Reducing the enemy to subhuman qualities allows us to abuse or kill them with greater ease. Reducing opponents to Ragheads, Gooks, Krauts, or Nips who do not have personal names like us allows them to become faceless, less-than-human characters who wear strange clothes, eat repugnant foods, and follow customs and religious practices that are different from our own and strange to us. Many atrocities in war emerge out of this sense of cultural distance where we see the other as animals, insects, or vermin. Once the enemy is seen in this way, such acts as killing prisoners, abusing civilians, or burning homes and pillaging neighborhoods becomes thinkable and doable.

Moral Distance

Moral distance involves legitimizing oneself and one's cause. It can generally be divided into two components. The first component usually is the determination and condemnation of the enemy's guilt, which of course must be punished or avenged. The other is an affirmation of the legality and legitimacy of one's own cause. Moral distance establishes that the enemy's cause is clearly wrong, his leaders are criminal, and his soldiers are either simply misguided or are sharing in their leader's guilt. But the enemy is still human, and killing him is an act of justice rather than the extermination that is often motivated by cultural distance. (Grossman, 1996, p. 164)

Integral to the revenge and seeking justice motive is a lack of desire to know all the facts before taking action. Most wars are like divorces between couples—they have long histories of accumulated offenses and slights that eventually boil over into one party doing something so overt that the other party can't stand the relationship anymore and "goes to war" to right all the wrongs perpetrated against them. Rarely are wars the product of a guilty party and an innocent party. Both parties have taken positions of being on the high moral ground. Neither party has very good habits of compromise and quickly shifts into a game of "I win/you lose." Both see themselves as right and the other as wrong. Then it is only a matter of time before one party makes a preemptive strike to win the conflict. If they fail in that attempt, a war of revenge for that act ensues, with devastating and costly results for all parties.

Macro-ethical/Political Issues Affecting Veterans Later in Life

Another ethical struggle comes when killing is done, but the cause for which one is fighting is ambiguous. Looking back, these veterans can't seem to justify their actions on grounds of defending themselves or stopping a greater evil. Was it a war of national aggression waged for money or power? Veterans ask themselves these questions, and if the answer is yes, they may then feel that they have been used to do the bidding of powerful and aggressive political and business leaders who did not have the purest motives in going to war. It is a lot harder for veterans to try to justify in their own minds the taking of people's lives for such causes. Years after a conflict, the propaganda wanes and truth seeps out, and veterans are haunted even more. Colonial wars and armed conflicts for political influence and power have been fought historically on this basis.

MG Smedley D. Butler, USMC, who has a U.S. Marine base in Okinawa, Japan, named after him (Marine Corps Base Camp S. D. Butler), was awarded the Medal of Honor twice for military actions. In 1935, after his retirement, he expressed his disgust and disillusionment at his moral failure in having participated in many wars that were fought primarily for American business interests at the turn of the twentieth century:

> I spent 33 years and four months in active military service and during that period I spent most of my time as a high-class muscle man for Big Business, for Wall Street, and the bankers. In short, I was a racketeer, a gangster for capitalism. I helped make Mexico and especially Tampico safe for American oil interests in 1914. I helped make Haiti and Cuba a decent place for the National City Bank boys to collect revenues in. I helped in the raping of half a dozen Central American republics for the benefit of Wall Street. Looking back on it, I might have given Al Capone a few hints. (Butler, 1935)

Involvement in such military actions corrodes the hearts and minds of ethically minded veterans. They are uncomfortable about their participation in such wars for years after their service. Many veterans of such wars were not proud of what they did and wanted little to do with the military or to talk about their military service. They experienced moral and spiritual trauma fighting for causes that were not just or were based on false pretenses. Such service does violence to the souls of soldiers, leaving them cynical and bitter for having served causes not worthy of honorable warriors' sacrifices. A war for profit or power, not based on solid moral ground or in defense of one's country, damages a soldier's values and self-esteem. That soldier is placed at risk of becoming a moral casualty in wars like these.

Concluding Thoughts: Grace and Forgiveness for Moral Failure

Edward Tick, in writing *Bringing Our Wounded Warriors Home*, says:

> War is inherently a moral enterprise and veterans in search of healing are on a profound moral journey. Our veterans cannot heal unless society accepts its responsibility for its war making. To the returning veteran, our leaders and people must say, "You did this in our name and because you were subject to our orders. We lift the burden of your actions from you and take it on our shoulders. We are responsible for you, for what you did (in our name), and for the consequences." (Tick, 2008, p. 3).

Especially in our public remembrance of veterans' sacrifices, we can acknowledge our role as a people in electing and supporting leaders who called soldiers to go to war in our name. We can, in these moments of humility, acknowledge our need of grace and forgiveness and create "grace space" for veterans to come to peace with their own moral struggles with war.

None of us lives a perfect life. We all have sinned and fallen short of the glory of God. The good news is that God's grace and forgiveness reaches out to us when we quit making excuses and rationalizations for missing the mark. Like the psalmist in Psalm 51, we ask for God's mercy to blot out our transgressions and wash away all our iniquity and cleanse us from sin. We can count on God to renew our spirit and restore unto us the joy of our salvation.

Soldiers, like all of us, sin. They, like us, can miss the mark of being all that God wants them to be. They know the seven deadly sins as well as we do. They too need to experience the grace and love of God to make new beginnings.

Veterans who make mistakes in battle, or who do things that in retrospect they would like to undo, can struggle for years over these lapses. For some who have taken lives or done other things in war that haunt them, there is a need for forgiveness or absolution for actions taken. They need to hear the words of Psalm 103:

> Praise the LORD, Oh my soul and forget not all his benefits—who forgives all your sins and heals all your diseases, who redeems your life from the pit and crowns you with love and compassion. . . . The LORD is compassionate and gracious, slow to anger, abounding in love. . . . He does not treat us as our sins deserve or repay us according to our iniquities. For as high as the heavens are above the earth, so great is his love for those who fear him; as far as the east is from the west, so far has he removed our transgressions from us. (Psalm 103:2-4, 8, 10-12 NIV)

Tips for Ministry

- Understand some of the ethical challenges facing service personnel, provide a listening ear for them to deal with their feelings, and consider issues of war and peace with them.
- Study the basic Christian positions on war and peace so that you can be a helpful resource for a service person seeking guidance on ethical issues and actions.
- With veterans who are struggling with moral or ethical failure due to their wartime service, share the gospel of grace and forgiveness to help them become liberated from guilt and spiritual alienation.
- Think through your own beliefs, attitudes, and assumptions. How do these influence your care of soldiers and their families?

CHAPTER SEVEN

Putting Feet to Our Faith: Creating a Military Family-friendly Church

"When, Lord, did we ever see you hungry and feed you, or thirsty and give you a drink? When did we ever see you a stranger and welcome you in our homes, or naked and clothe you? When did we ever see you sick or in prison, and visit you? The King will reply, 'I tell you, whenever you did this for one of the least important of these followers of mine, you did it for me!' "
—Matthew 25:37-40 GNT

Being good neighbors, people who love others as themselves, starts with an ability to see people in need. One way to develop this kind of vision is by traveling to places where people are in great need. Once we see poverty, malnutrition, and disease, we are challenged personally to take some responsibility to meet those needs; the vision becomes the mission. Jesus remarks that this attitude of reaching out to those in need should become such a reflexive thing that people hardly recognize they are doing anything really important or out of the ordinary. It is just something that people who call themselves Disciples of Christ do naturally as part of their faith expression.

When it comes to reaching out to military families and returning veterans, many churches mean well but don't see the needs; they don't travel in circles that allow them to know families with someone in uniform. They don't have enough knowledge of military life to have a clue about the needs of veterans and their families or how to minister to them. They find themselves asking, "When, Lord, did we see you in need?"

Most churches would help, if they knew the needs of veterans and their families and how to appropriately respond to them. This is best illustrated by a story of two churches.

Tale of Two Churches

One church wanted to be a military-friendly church, since it was located near a large military base. In spite of their best intentions, church leaders and members saw military families as transient and peripheral to their ministry. They were seen as "regular visitors" at services but were not often invited into leadership or support roles in the church. After all, they would be gone to another duty station in two or three years; how could the church build around them? The result was that the relationships this church had with military families remained superficial, and church leaders had little understanding of the challenges military families faced.

One Sunday the pastor introduced a regular attendee, a senior noncommissioned officer, and made a presentation of a "Hawaiian shirt." The NCO was being ordered to a one-year unaccompanied tour to Diego Garcia (a small island in the Indian Ocean) without his family. This was hardly a moment to celebrate for either him or his family. He was in his final year of military service, and the assignment was not given to him as a favor. The pastor made it seem like the serviceman was going on a fantastic vacation, disregarding the family who were sitting in that church, painfully contemplating that year of separation. Military families in the congregation winced at the presentation and felt sorry for this family. They also knew that this pastor and this church were clueless about the needs or the painful challenges military families faced. It was a spiritually alienating experience for service members in the pews.

A second church, also located in an area with large numbers of service personnel, was much more sensitive, innovative, and inclusive. Military families were welcomed and expected to become contributing members in the stewardship of time, talent, and finances.

Those who could teach were asked to teach in the church's religious education programs; those who could lead and administrate were called upon to do so. There was a wonderful blending of civilian and military in the body of Christ in that congregation. People got to relate as fellow pilgrims, grappling with common issues regardless of vocation.

The messages from the pulpit addressed real issues that people face in challenging times, concerns not unique to military personnel, but those dealing with cancer, divorce, unemployment, disability, and child-rearing. The pastor preached the truth about life and death issues and equipped the congregation spiritually to face adversity with courage and faith. People came away from services inspired and motivated to contextualize the truths of the message in whatever context they lived.

It was not a superpatriotic or nationalistic church, but it honored the service and sacrifices of military families and fully appreciated some of the ethical tensions and practical challenges service personnel faced on issues of war and peace. Those in uniform were not stereotyped as militaristic types but rather seen as individuals who held a wide variety of opinions on the armed conflicts we faced. Military personnel and their families felt respected and felt safe to belong and become in that faith community.

The care and outreach ministries in this church included military families, as their outreach encompassed all families. The church had a regular "Mom's Morning Out" program where those with young children could participate in a morning of activities, with childcare provided, and fellowship with other moms to receive a short respite from "the daily-ness" of childcare responsibilities. Especially for military moms temporarily acting as single parents, this was a special blessing. Some of the church ministries were more unscheduled and informal: for example, fixing a flat tire or broken kitchen window; inviting children with deployed parents to join another church family in a trip to the beach or amusement park; or helping out with soccer and softball practice; or even making sure that military kids got on the teams church members coached.

There was a personal kind of thoughtfulness and love in that church. One day a woman in the church invited my wife and our three preschool boys to come and choose from the 39 flavors in her ice cream store. She did not know my wife was feeling a little sad and lonely. Neither did she know that that very day was my wife's birthday, but the Lord knew, and she knew the Lord. She was sensitive enough to the Spirit of God to be prompted on that day to reach out to my wife in love and encourage her in Jesus' name. It made a huge difference in my wife's life and created a lasting memory.

None of these people, in this military-family-friendly church, saw any of these acts as a "big deal." Rather, they saw their actions as just part of ordinary Christian living in a community committed to seeking to love God with all their heart and their neighbors as themselves. The cumulative effect of all these acts of kindness for my family by many people was enormous, and thirty years later we haven't forgotten the kind of love they showed us in our time together. When we start to feel cynical about something we see going wrong in the church today, we remember these times with this congregation, who not only talked the talk but also walked the walk. They put feet to their faith and showed their faith through their good works when they acted on behalf of God "to the least of these."

Characteristics of a Military Family-friendly Church

How does a congregation become this kind of military-friendly church? It takes some thoughtful consideration of a few basic principles to reach out to military families and veterans to draw them into the circumference of a church's ministry.

Being Inclusive toward Soldiers and Their Families

Churches are sometimes not as welcoming as they think they are. They have erected barriers that make it hard for "outsiders" to feel welcome. For example, political views might get in the way of caring for military families or veterans. Soldiers may be blamed for a particular foreign policy and so not be recognized as our fellow citizens who are simply doing their duty by serving. Most service personnel will serve under many commanders in chief from both political parties during their career and have little influence over the policies of the leaders elected. Military personnel who are members of the church may hold wide-ranging political views; all have a right to be included in our ministry plans.

The church is more than a building on the corner of Ninth and Vine; it is more than a closely knit group of people who don't need any more friends. Leaders are tasked with building a community of Christian believers, first, equipped for ministry in the church's gathered phase, and then dispersed into the larger community to serve.

One challenge is to find military families who live in civilian communities, attend public schools, play on youth athletic teams, and work at local places of employment. These service members and their families may not automatically show up at local churches. Soldiers and their families aren't likely to jump out of bed on a Sunday morning, hoping to hear a well-rehearsed choir or listen to a good sermon. There are service personnel and military family members who attend church regularly, but, like civilians their age, the majority of soldiers in their twenties and thirties do not attend churches. In order to find these soldiers and their families, the church has to offer relevant ministries that meet their needs in teachable moments of their lives. The next step is to advertise these services and programs to make them visible.

Having Challenging Service Opportunities for Soldiers and Their Families

Soldiers and their families want to be challenged by tasks that are worth doing, rather than become mere spectators or consumers. Once the word gets out in the military and veteran community that certain churches are welcoming others, people will want to become part of that ministry and it will flourish.

Military families and veterans know what it is to sacrifice for a cause greater than themselves. While many civilians respond to appeals out of self-interest and "What will it profit me?" veterans and their families respond more positively to a cause that will make a difference in the world. This selflessness is much closer to the heart of God and more in line with the commandment to love your neighbor as yourself. Some veterans have seen firsthand how soldiers lay down their lives for one another.

As previously noted, soldiers and their families have needs, yet they also have much to offer a church, given the chance to be a part of the community of faith. In a study of "military brats," some of the traits learned in the service and found in military families are exactly the kind of characteristics a church needs to be successful. Mary Edwards Wertsch lists these traits in her book *Military Brats*:

Responsibleness (they take the notion of duty very seriously), **excellent social skills** (they get along with almost anybody), **resilience** (they cope with almost anything), **loyalty** (it is hard for anyone to outshine them here), **willingness to take risks** (able to leap into a new and challenging situation), **discipline** (they enjoy controlling and focusing their energies to become extremely productive and efficient), **tolerance** (they can adapt to many situations, cultures, and different points of view), **idealism** (they can be extremely dedicated to matters of principle and go to extraordinary lengths to promote or defend them), and **handling a crisis well** (they often handle emergencies with calm and confidence). (Wertsch, 1991, pp. 395-96)

Service members, spouses, retired military personnel, and veterans—as well as military brats—have many of these traits and have much to offer a church. They can be valuable participants in the community of faith.

Sometimes church leaders observe the coming and going of active duty, reserve, and National Guard personnel and question their usefulness to the church's Christian education and other programs. Yes, the church may need to be a bit more flexible in order to encourage participation of military families, but the church has much to gain by including military personnel and their spouses in teaching religious education, inviting them to be on committees, or selecting them for board assignments.

Churches could challenge veterans to do great tasks and find new meaning and vision for their lives through, for example, working alongside others to build houses for the homeless, fighting for justice, going on mission trips to build clinics or schools, participating in recovery programs with prisoners, drug addicts, or the mentally ill (many of whom are veterans). Getting veterans off the bench as spectators and getting them involved in ministry will ignite their hearts to do great things for God, just as they did great things for their country.

Speaking to Needs of Soldiers and Their Families

The best preaching and teaching ministries of the church grapple with real problems of soldiers, veterans, and military families as they continue to serve or as they recover from the wounds of war. This does not mean creating a new program for soldiers only. But it does mean awareness by pastors and leaders of how themes of guilt and grace, grief and loss, courage and integrity, hurt and forgiveness may have a larger meaning to service members and their families. It also means speaking to some of the issues faced by returning veterans and their families, dealing with wounds of mind, body, and spirit. It calls for being theologically robust in dealing with the big issues of life and death with people who regularly go in harm's way and being spiritually vibrant enough to grow disciples of Christ who can become "salt" and "light" in the dark places of the world where they are asked to go.

Having a Supportive Community

Going through a deployment or through the reintegration process after a war is hard to do. Even more difficult is for a wounded veteran and his or her family to recover from the wounds of war. The most painful thing for a grieving family to do is to lay to rest a son or daughter, husband or wife, mother or dad who made the ultimate sacrifice for the country. None of these service members and their families or survivors should have to face these challenges alone. The church can be at its best here and show what it is to love the neighbor as oneself, both in word and action. Organizing congregations into small-group ministries whose members encourage one another in difficult times is an ideal way to support military families. It is the well-timed helping hand, the kind word of encouragement, the supporting presence in times of loneliness and struggle that will make a lasting difference in the lives of military families and veterans.

Practical Ideas for Helping

As church leaders become aware of the various struggles found within military families, they almost inevitably ask, "But how can we specifically help? How can we meet the needs we have become aware of?" There is no "right way" to reach out to military families, but there are guidelines that can help churches succeed in this very important ministry.

1. Be specific when you offer help: Don't say, "Please call me when you need something." You will never be called. Rather, say, "I am bringing a meal to your house Friday night at 5:00 unless I hear different from you."
2. Be creative in how you help: Soldiers enjoy getting phone cards and various toiletries. But families at home enjoy getting things too. Families with young children appreciate gift certificates to restaurants or movie passes or specific offers to babysit.
3. Ask what military families need: Don't assume that you know what they need or when they need it. Soldiers in the desert don't need care packages filled with melted chocolates. They don't need electronics when they have limited access to electricity.
4. Be OK when a family declines an offer: If a military family says they don't need your help *at this time*, please remain supportive. They may not need that meal now or that offer of babysitting today, but that does not mean they won't need it in the future. Offers of help are always appreciated, even when assistance is not currently needed.

Churches are in the unique position of being able to draw on a committed group of volunteers who are used to helping others. Some churches have formal military ministries and hold regular meetings. Other churches promote specific military projects, while others try to educate congregants on how to do general outreach to all people, including those touched by the military.

Family Assistance Centers (FACs) and Family Readiness Groups (FRGs)

FACs are found in each state. They are intended to be a point of contact for all military families and usually are formed for major deployments. Their purpose is primarily to provide information and to help families link to needed resources. However, they also support families directly through services such as emergency financial assistance, family enrollment in military-sponsored insurance, and linkage to various military benefits.

FRGs are Family Readiness Groups, which are activated when there is an impending deployment. FRGs are a volunteer-based support network that brings families together on a regular basis, both prior to and during a deployment. Leaders are often spouses of deployed soldiers. These groups offer training, education, and support for families.

Both FRGs and FACs are aware of families with various needs. Churches can notify local FRGs and FACs to let them know what services or support they can give military families. In turn, the FRGs and FACs can link families they know to the services they need.

For example, a military spouse may break a leg while her husband is away. Because she is functionally a single mom for one year, she now faces some new challenges. She has a broken leg *and* she also has four young children. How does she get the older children to school? How does she get to the grocery store on a weekly basis? She is told by the military to let her FRG and FAC know of any struggles she experiences during the deployment. If she goes to the local FAC with this challenge, the local FAC is responsible for finding help for her. If the FAC is aware of church volunteers or organized care programs like Stephen or

BeFrienders Ministries, then the FAC specialist can call the church and discuss the current situation and work with the church to find appropriate volunteers.

Specific Ideas for Military Outreach

There are literally hundreds of ideas on how to support military families during the deployment cycle. Most churches do a combination of activities. Some may have a bulletin board in their narthex that has pictures of all current service men and women. Others may designate a Sunday that focuses on the military to honor those who serve. Quilting groups can join together to make blankets for deployed soldiers. Sunday school groups may collect phone cards to send to service members all over the world. Churches will individually decide what works best for them and the families they seek to serve.

Pre-deployment

- Meet and greet: Find out who in your community or congregation are deploying. Let them know you are aware of the upcoming deployment and will be available to help as needed. This allows the entire family to build trust with you prior to the deployment. Many soldiers feel relieved when they know there is someone back home who is helping care for their loved ones.
- Offer time away: Many military families feel that they never have enough time to prepare for a deployment, especially if they have children. Many couples would benefit from a night or a weekend away to talk about their concerns and questions. Give them an "away gift" when their children are watched and a hotel or bed-and-breakfast is pre-paid so they can go away and spend uninterrupted time together.

During Deployment

- Adopt a Soldier: "My Soldier" is a program that lets U.S. troops know that someone back home cares. This is a no-cost program. Once you enroll, you will receive a starter kit containing a red My Soldier bracelet that publicly shows your support for American troops. This can be given to youth groups, Sunday school classes, or the entire church. http://www.mysoldier.com
- USO Care Package Program: This program was created to provide a safe and secure way for the public to show their support and care for our men and women in uniform. The USO is a congressionally chartered nonprofit corporation whose mission is to provide morale, welfare, and recreation services to military personnel. For a small donation, Americans can sponsor a care package for a service member who is currently deployed. www.usocares.org
- Project Home Front: While our troops take care of our homeland, we can help take care of their homes. This concentrated effort helps families keep up their homes while their loved ones are away. You can volunteer, start an affiliate, or help in many other ways. http://www.projecthomefont.org
- A Million Thanks: This is a year-round campaign to show U.S. military men and women, past and present, your appreciation for their sacrifices, dedication, and services to your country through letters, e-mails, cards, prayers, and thoughts. http://www.AmillionThanks.org
- Cell Phones for Soldiers: Donated cell phones go to recyclers. The income generated goes to purchase calling cards for our troops. http://www.cellphonesforsoldiers.com
- Operation Paperback: Donate slightly used paperbacks to our troops. This provides easy and

mobile entertainment. http://operationpaper
back.usmilitarysupport.org

• Blankets of Hope: People are needed to sew blankets for the thousands of wounded soldiers in our
country or in hospitals abroad. These blankets
offer ongoing comfort and warmth.
http://soldiersangels.org

• Information from your church: Make sure the soldier is receiving the bulletin and newsletter from
his or her home church. Downloadable sermons
are also appreciated.

The following highlights ideas for reaching out to military families:

• Operation Honey Do: This organization is a group
of handymen who assist family members whose
regular problem fixers are deployed. They can fix
basic plumbing, repair screen doors, stain a deck,
and so forth. Consider joining a local organization
or starting your own. http://www.operation
honeydo.com/

• Care Packages for Families at home: Pack a care
package with gift certificates, movie passes, and
homemade food. These can also be tailored to current holidays.

• Include stay-at-home families in your outings.
Invite them to go on a picnic, go fishing, or go
along to an amusement park.

• Mow their lawns or do other things to help them
take care of their yard and home. Rake leaves,
shovel snow, or pull weeds.

• Offer a listening ear:

1. Check in: Find out how they are doing through
cards, e-mails, or phone calls.
2. Encourage the person to talk about his or her
loved one who has been deployed.

3. Remember that holidays and birthdays can be especially tough for the person left at home.

Post-deployment

• Stay connected: Most of the time the needs of families lessen when their loved one is home. But staying connected offers ongoing support and friendship.

Concluding Thoughts

Becoming a military and veteran family-friendly church is about being a servant church that sees military families and veterans as neighbors in need and seeks to reach out to them in a time of need. The words of "The Servant Song" encapsulate the spirit of such a church, which seeks to "love our neighbor as ourselves." May the words of this song help us dedicate ourselves to serve veterans and their families who have served our country in time of need:

I will hold the Christ-light for you . . .
    speak the peace you long to hear.
(Gillard, 1977)

References

Bannerman, Stacy. "Broken Marriages: Another Casualty of War." AlterNet, www.alternet.com, January 23, 2009.

Butler, Smedly D. *War Is a Racket*. New York: Round Table Press, 1935.

Department of Defense Personnel & Procurement Statistics, April 2009.

Falk, Richard. "Defining a Just War," *The Nation*, October 11, 2001.

Gilliard, Richard. "The Servant Song." Scripture in Song-Division of Integrity Music, 1977.

Grossman, Dave. *On Killing*. New York: Back Bay Books, 1996.

Independent Budget for Fiscal Year 2009, Department of Veterans Affairs: Washington, DC.

Internet Database of Memorable Quotes. *Apocalypse Now* (1979).

Military Human Resources Strategic Plan. Office of Undersecretary of Defense for Personnel and Readiness (2009).

National Military Family Association Survey (2005).

Preliminary Report of the Psychological Needs of the US Military Service Members and Their Families, TF Report (2006).

Ramirez, Jessica. "Children of Conflict," *Newsweek*, June 15, 2009.

RAND, National Defense Research Institute (2008).

Roth-Douquet, Kathy. "More Than a Long Weekend," *USA Today*, May 21, 2009.

Stone, Daniel, Eve Connant, and John Barry. "Love Is a Battlefield," *Newsweek* magazine, June 15, 2009.

Taylor, Richard H. *Homeward Bound: American Veterans Return from War.* Westport, CT: Praeger Security International, 2007.

Tick, Edward. "Bringing Our Wounded Warriors Home," www.SoldiersHeart.net (2008).

Thielike, Helmut. *The Waiting Father.* New York: Harper and Bros. Publishers, 1959.

Thompson, Mark. "The Wounded Come Home," *Time* magazine, November 3, 2003.

Veterans Affairs, *PTSD and the Family Booklet* (2006).

Wertsch, Mary E. *Military Brats: Legacies of Childhood Inside the Fortress.* New York: Harmony Books, 1991.

Worden, William J. *Grief Counseling & Grief Therapy: A Handbook for the Mental Health Practitioner.* New York: Springer Publishing Company, 1991.

Wounded Warrior Program (Dec. 2008), www.aw2.army.mil/family corner/index.

About the Authors

Chaplain (CDR) David A. Thompson, CHC, USNR (Ret.) is a Licensed Professional Counselor (LPC) who assists deploying and returning soldiers and their families. He and his family have experienced several deployments with both the Navy and Marine Corps and he knows the challenges of coming home after war. David is an ordained minister with the Free Methodist Church of North America and was endorsed to serve on active duty as a Navy chaplain by the Free Methodist Church and the United Methodist Division on Chaplains and Related Ministries.

Darlene F. Wetterstrom is a Licensed Independent Clinical Social Worker (LICSW) who has extensive experience working with children and families in a variety of settings, including the military. Darlene is an active member of Woodbury / Peaceful Grove United Methodist Church, Woodbury, Minnesota, where her husband serves as senior pastor.